MARY IN AN ADULT CHURCH

BEYOND DEVOTION TO RESPONSE

by

Father David M. Knight

Copyright © 1988 by David M. Knight
All rights reserved
ISBN # 0-942971-11-6

His Way Communications
1992

TABLE OF CONTENTS

PREFACE

Why another book on Mary? What kind of book will this be?

The kind of book I intend this to be is the reason for writing it. There are devotional books on Mary and doctrinal books on Mary and books which combine the two. This is meant as a book on Mary which invites us to *respond* to what we believe about Mary -- to respond to it in *choices* that lift up the level of our response to Jesus Christ.

Everything the Church teaches about Mary is really a teaching about Jesus or about the Church -- that is, about us and about the life we are called to live as the body of Christ on earth. To understand the mystery of Mary is to understand the mystery of the Incarnation and the mystery of living the life of grace. This is what makes her so dear to us.

I am not suggesting that we love Mary only because she is a theological wedge! It is true that her unique reality is a key for opening up the mystery of Christ and of our own life in Christ, but we do not love her just for that, the way a researcher loves his reference

1

book! We love Mary because in her we see the feminine side of God. We see God in her expressing Himself to us as a woman, being a woman for us. We love Mary because of the way she helps us know God's love for us and makes it easier for us to love Him back. We love her because she loves us and because her love is both human and divine, because by grace she is both human and divine -- just the way we are. We love Mary because in her, as in each one of us, God is made flesh again -- by the "grace of Our Lord Jesus Christ" which we proclaim as the theme of our celebration every morning at Mass.

In Mary God is our Mother, God is our sister and the woman we love. And the deep doctrinal teaching on Mary which makes us able to say these shocking things about her (and they are shocking; we should make no bones about that) makes us able to accept the shocking statements we are called to make about ourselves: that through grace each one of us becomes a revelation of God on earth: a revelation of God, not just as male or female, but as old or young, healthy or sick, genius or retarded -- yes, even as innocent or wounded by sin! We are not just mothers and fathers, brothers and sisters to one another; in each one of us Jesus Christ is being father or mother, brother or sister, friend, companion or spouse to other people. When we say that God the Son, the Second Person of the Blessed Trinity, took flesh in Mary's womb, we are led inevitably to accept the fact that through the gift of grace He has also taken flesh in us. And when we say that Mary is the Mother of God, we have to continue with logical consistency to the recognition that we ourselves have become through baptism the body, the flesh of God on earth. (Since this is just an introduction, we won't take time to develop these ideas here. They will be clarified in later chapters).

We love Mary because she reveals the feminine side of God to us. But in doing so she also reveals the divine side of each one of us -- and makes us realize that we are each revealing to one another that particular face of God which can only be reflected by the particular, the unique humanity that belongs to each one of us. If in Mary, because she was "full of grace,"we see what God would have been like incarnated as a woman, then in every person who is a visible embodiment of the "grace of Our Lord Jesus Christ," and in the measure that each one is surrendered to living by that grace, we see what God would have been like incarnated in a different way.

Once we accept this -- that we are not just followers of Jesus, but that each one of us is His real presence, His continuing human and divine, saving presence on earth -- we are faced with what this calls us to be and to do for one another. If we are not just followers of Jesus, but if we are in a real sense Jesus Himself, His real and risen body on earth, then how are we called to be and to act toward the Father? Toward Jesus our head? Toward the Holy Spirit? What are we called to be for one another, and how can we grow into being it? How can we grow into being for God and for each other what Jesus is? What Mary is? What each one of us is called to be?

That is what this book is all about. It is a very practical book. Its aim is to enlighten our minds in order to challenge our hearts. It is to let us see what we are called to be so that we will devote ourselves with clearer understanding, more awestruck faith, and a more excited hope to the task of "building up the body of Christ in love," beginning with ourselves. We look at Mary in order to be what Mary is: to let the Word and the words of God take flesh in us.

The inspiration and basic outline of this book both come from a brilliant class taught at Fourvière, in Lyon, France, by Father Joseph Moignt, S.J. In that class he showed how the mysteries of the Immaculate Conception and Virgin Birth were necessary preparations for Mary's principal role as *Theotokos* or Mother of God. And from this central dogma -- that Mary is the Mother of God -- it follows with logical consistency that she was ever sinless and "full of grace," and that her body was taken up into heaven without undergoing the corruption of the grave (the doctrine of the Assumption). Consequently, this book begins with the central doctrine, that Mary is Mother of God, then takes up the mysteries presupposed for this -- the Virgin Birth and the Immaculate Conception -- and then looks at the doctrines that follow from the fact that Mary is Mother of God: that she was "ever virgin," "ever sinless," "full of grace" and assumed into heaven. Above all, this book focuses on what these mysteries call us to choose and to be in our lives.

HOW TO USE THIS BOOK
Helps for Reflection and Response

There are levels of investment in the reading of this book. The more one chooses to invest, of course, the more one will get out of the book.

• *First level of investment:* Read the book.

• *Second level:* In addition, spend some time on each chapter praying over the theme of the chapter, using the helps at the end of each chapter -- for example, the Scripture text, reflection questions and Prayerform.

• *Third level:* Meet with someone to discuss each chapter and to decide how to embody in your lives whatever new understanding the theme of the chapter has led you to.

TO HELP YOU, you will find at the end of each chapter some tools for "Reflection and Response." They consist in:

A SCRIPTURE TEXT: A way to pray over Scripture is just to read the passage, being alert to whatever word, image or idea draws your attention or moves you the most, and then to ask yourself what meaning it has for you in your life and what you can do to live it out. Talk to God silently in your own words if you feel like it. *For example,* read the *Magnificat*, Luke 1:46-55 and ask yourself what kind of woman Mary is.

PRAYER (*different with each chapter*): Mary, guide me through this book. Let your being proclaim to me the greatness of the Lord. Let my generation call you blessed and see in you the blessings God has given to us with His grace, that we might love Him more and open

6

our hearts more to all that He is and wishes us to be for us. Pray with me for this to Christ our Lord. *Amen*.

AN OBJECTIVE for each chapter: The key to this book is *understanding, appreciating* and *responding*. We want to understand on a deep and solid theological level what Mary is for us, not just in terms of felt devotion, but in terms of what the Church believes and teaches. And we want to love her, not just as children love their mother, but as adults who understand her and appreciate what the reality of her life calls us to be. Finally, we want to respond, and to live our Christian lives in greater length and breadth and height and depth because of what we see and love in her. We want to understand the mystery of her life, love what she is, and live out what she stands for. For each chapter, the theme and goal of the chapter is spelled out to facilitate response.

INVENTORY: The purpose of this part of the *Reflection and Response* pages is just to see what you already know or have experienced. There are no "right" or "wrong" answers, just information. For example, ask yourself now:

- What did Mary mean to you when you were little? How did you interact with her then?
- What does Mary mean to you now? How do you interact or deal with her now?
- What is the best thing Mary has done or been for you in your life?

INPUT: These are some questions to help you pinpoint what you have gotten out of reading the chapter.

INITIATIVE: Each time you read a chapter, take some time for personal, reflection and decision-making. Try to decide on some practical, concrete choice inspired by the chapter. This is the moment when faith turns into response; when understanding and appreciation are expressed in action. If the doctrine on Mary that you have been considering has taken root in your heart, then it should bear fruit in choices. The initiative section of the chapter is a time to get in touch with what one particular doctrine means to yourself, and what it should mean in your life. To get started, in response to this introduction ask yourself:

- Do I want to make this program? Why?
- What do I want to ask of Mary during it? What will I give her?
- In practical terms of time and space, when can I do the reading? When and where can I reflect and pray over it?
- Is there a time and place in which I can give ten minutes to praying according to the prayer form suggested with each chapter?
- Is there anyone with whom I could meet to discuss each chapter and to make decisions about how to apply these topics to life?

PRAYER FORM: Choose a time and a place that allow you to be completely undisturbed for ten minutes. During this time use the Prayerform suggested for each chapter. At the end of the period talk to Mary in your own words if you desire. Do this each time you read a chapter.

MANTRA: This is just a phrase to repeat frequently during the day in order to keep aware of what you are doing during these days.

CHAPTER ONE
"MOTHER OF GOD"

The Church made a dogma out of the word "*Theotokos*" (in Latin *Dei Genetrix*, in English "Mother of God") at the Council of Ephesus in the year 431. What does that mean to us today?

First of all, what does it mean to say that a doctrine has become a dogma? The word "doctrine" just means "teaching." And teaching can be rather vague and imprecise until someone starts asking specific questions. But when questions force the Church to get more precise about what she believes and teaches, dogma is born. And this is what we mean by a "dogma." It is a carefully worded, precise statement of belief that is usually made necessary by a furious debate which has sprung up over questions not explicitly asked or answered in Scripture.

When the Church clarifies her teaching with dogmas, therefore, it is a sign that the People of God are alive and questioning, probing into the deeper meaning of their faith; and that authorities in the Church are encouraging and responding to this. Paradoxically, the more dogmas the Church comes up with, the less "dogmatic" her spirit is in the popular, frozen interpretation of the word.

"Mother of God"

The Church always taught, as a doctrine or general teaching right out of Scripture, that Mary was the mother of Jesus. Then someone asked, "Is it correct to say that, since Jesus is God, Mary is the mother of God?" That didn't sound right. After all, God existed before Mary did, and God is the creator. How could a creature be the mother of the creator? And so some people suggested that we should call Mary the mother of Jesus' humanity only, but not of Jesus as God. Or say that she was the mother of His body, but not of Jesus as a person.

The Church's answer to this focused right on the mystery of Jesus, not of Mary. The conclusion of the debates was that Jesus must not be divided. We must not, in speaking of Jesus, divide His humanity from His divinity or His body from the rest of Him. Jesus is Jesus, with everything He is. And just as we do not say that our own mothers are just the mothers of our bodies (although they did not produce our spiritual souls but God creates each person's soul directly) neither can we say that Mary was just the mother of a part of Jesus. Being His mother, she was the mother of His person. And since the person of Jesus is God, the Second Person of the Blessed Trinity, Mary is the mother of God.

We are the "body of Christ"

This might sound rather abstract. But when we start thinking about what it means for us it gets practical very fast. We call ourselves -- because St. Paul says it repeatedly -- the "body of Christ" on earth (see, for example, Romans 12:1-8; 1 Corinthians 12:12-31; Ephesians 4:1-16). What does that mean? Does it mean that when we act as Jesus' body, Jesus Himself is acting? God is acting? Or should we say that when we, as members of Christ, do something, it is only the body of Jesus that is acting -- not the divine person of Jesus Himself?

When the Church teaches and governs, is Jesus Himself teaching and governing, or just His human body? When we show love for one another -- for our family, our friends,

the people we work with or work for -- are
these acts divine or merely human? When
parents raise their children, is Jesus doing
this in them, or do the parents just do it as
His body -- that is, as His human body dis-
tinct and apart from His divinity as God?

The answer is still that Jesus cannot be divided. The Church argues that if Mary is the
mother of Jesus, she is the mother of all He
is; therefore she is the Mother of God. In the
same way, if we are the body of Christ, we are
the body of Jesus the person, and therefore
we are the body of God. Our flesh is the flesh
of God. We are divine. When we act as the
body of Christ on earth, Jesus the divine person of God is acting in us. Whatever the
Church does in grace, Jesus is doing.

For those of you who are inclined to ask theological questions faster than I can make theological distinctions, let us just note that, yes,
there is a difference between the identity of
Jesus with the body He was born with and
His identification with us who are His body
now. We are hardly in danger of forgetting
that difference. The danger for us is to forget
how real our oneness with Jesus is. We need
to take seriously the depth and mystery of
our union with Him as His real body on

earth. We need to understand that although Jesus the divine person can be distinguished from us as His body on earth, He must not be divided from us. We are truly the body of Jesus Christ. [1]

Asking a question about Mary led the Church to answer a question about Jesus. And understanding more clearly the mystery of Mary has led us to see more clearly the mystery of ourselves, of our own divine-human reality as united to Jesus by grace. We are the body, the real body of Jesus Christ on earth. What follows from that?

Partnership with Jesus

What follows is that in everything we do we act in partnership with Jesus. At baptism He said to each one of us, "Give me your body." St. Paul expressed it in his exhortation to the Roman Christians: "Offer your bodies as a living sacrifice to God!" (see Romans 12: 1-2).

---

[1] When God took Christ's human nature and body as His own, there was no created human person present. The person of Jesus is God the Son, the Second Person of the Blessed Trinity. When Jesus takes us as His body, both His person and ours are present acting in partnership.

13

A living sacrifice: it is our live bodies we offer to God, meaning our bodies and souls, our whole persons, with mind and heart and will. At baptism we accepted to be "sacrificed" to the work of God, to the interests and desires of Jesus, in everything we would do from that point on. Wherever our live bodies are, and whatever we are doing in them, we are pledged to sacrifice everything else to whatever it is that Jesus wants to do in us and through us at that moment. We are His body on earth. We are consecrated to this.

This is a true partnership. Partners act together. Neither one is just a passive instrument to be directed and used by the other. The body each one of us gave to Jesus is not inert. It is alive. We are still in it. We gave ourselves to live with Jesus in one flesh: to be two persons with one body; two persons united on the level of being, on the level of one shared life, and expressing themselves together in one flesh. Every graced human action we perform is the expression in human flesh of our own person and of Jesus, the infinite Son of God, acting together as one.

In everything we do as Jesus' body on earth, therefore, we must act with Him, in union with Him. We are not just robots, or bodies He "takes over" the way a driver takes over control of a car. Jesus will not act *in us* and *through us* unless *we act with Him*. We have to literally "co-operate" with Him in the active use of all our human faculties, especially our intellects and wills.

Our human cooperation required

In baptism Jesus calls us to be his partners, not His slaves. "I no longer call you servants," He said at the Last Supper, "but friends, because everything the Father has revealed to me, I have made known to you." Jesus wants us to act with Him. This means that if He wants to do something in and through us, it has to be something we are able to make a human decision about, something we are able to choose with Him.

This means it has to be something we are able to understand -- at least sufficiently to make an intelligent decision about it. Jesus never asks us (or allows us!) to just let ourselves be directed blindly by Him. Whatever He wants to do in us, He proposes it to our intellects and wills for our decision, the way one partner in a firm proposes something to another. Then we have the responsibility of saying "Yes" or "No." We have to make a decision in a responsible way, just as partners in a business have to take responsibility for understanding and approving every decision they vote for. Jesus won't have any "yes men."

We see this in the way God dealt with Mary when He asked her to be the mother of God. He asked her. She had to say "Yes." It had to be her choice, her free and responsible decision. And she had to understand what she was doing -- at least enough to choose it humanly and responsibly.

I am not denying that God calls us to make many decisions in faith, decisions about things we do not fully understand. Mary did this. She certainly did not understand the whole mystery of what she was being asked to become and do. But she did not consent blindly. She asked a question before she said yes: "How can this be done, since I am a virgin?" When the angel reassured her that the event would take place through the power of God acting on her directly, she made her choice: "I am the handmaid of the Lord. Let it be done to me according to your word."

This was still a surrender in faith. There were a dozen questions she still could have asked (and a dozen answers she could not have understood!) but she had enough knowledge to make a rational human decision. She knew enough to be able to surrender responsibly and to place her trust in God.

Because Jesus requires our human cooperation as His partners, the actual choice of what we will do or not do as His body is left to us. Jesus can inspire and move us from within to do something, but if we choose not to do it we can veto His motion. We can do nothing graced, of course, nothing that is truly divine unless He inspires it and acts through us. But we can refuse to do what He inspires us to do. And in that case the action just doesn't take place. Jesus is prevented from acting humanly on earth because we who are His partners and His body do not concur.

The key to the Catholic Church

I believe this is a key to the uniqueness of the Catholic religion: we take very seriously the doctrine that we are the body of Christ on earth. We believe in Jesus' real presence in His Church, just as we believe in His real presence in the Eucharist. There is a different kind of presence, a different kind of union in these two cases, of course, but both are equally real. We believe that Jesus not only has the power to change bread into His real body but that He also has the power and the love to come live in us and make us His real body.

I believe the Catholic Church is unique in her acceptance of the role human beings are called to play in the work of saving the world. We believe, of course, that only Jesus can save, and that no one can do anything graced or grace-giving unless in fact God Himself is the one who is doing it. We cannot even say "Yes" to an inspiration or grace of God except by the power of God. As St. Paul taught, no one can acknowledge Jesus as Lord or believe in Him -- no one can make the basic act of faith required to be a Christian -- except by the Holy Spirit (see 1 Corinthians 12:3). But Catholics believe that to give His grace on earth today Jesus truly works in and through His human body; that He communicates grace to people through the human actions that He performs in, through and with those who are united to Him as members of His body. He took a human nature to Himself in order to redeem the world, and

He continues His work of redemption on earth through the human natures of those who are joined to Him by grace.

For example, Catholics believe that Jesus truly forgives sins through the human words of forgiveness He speaks in the priest in the sacrament of reconciliation. And we believe Jesus truly gives Himself in spousal love through the words the bride and bridegroom say to each other in the sacrament of matrimony. Jesus Himself speaks these words and pledges His own self through them. We believe that when the priest anoints the sick Jesus Himself is anointing, touching and comforting. And when the priest says over bread and wine, "This is my body...this is my blood," it is Jesus Himself who is speaking. And so of all the sacraments.

Jesus acts in all the actions of His body

The sacraments are special, unique instances of Jesus acting through His body, but they are not the only way He does. The fact is, Catholics believe that in everything a member of the body of Christ does in grace, Jesus is acting. Jesus is smiling in those who smile. Jesus is nursing in those who nurse. Jesus is fixing cars in those who fix cars. Jesus is selling in those who sell and buying in those who buy. Jesus is making love in spouses who make love. On the assumption that all these actions are done in grace, Jesus is doing them in, through and with His body that is acting. He is our partner. He acts in partnership with us and we with Him. He is more than our partner: He is our head. We are one with Him in the sharing of one life. His is the body of which we are the members. He is the whole of which we are the parts.

Mary is the Mother of God: in and through her human act of giving birth to Jesus, God Himself took flesh as a human being. And we are the body of Christ: in and through our human actions Jesus Himself acts in human flesh on earth. This is our belief.

Mary and the Church

Awareness of Mary keeps us aware of what we are. As we accept and rejoice in the fact that she was truly Mother of God, we become more aware, with greater faith and deeper acceptance, that we are truly the body of Christ on earth. He who took flesh from Mary to become man has taken flesh from each one of us to continue His life and ministry on earth -- as man, as woman, as child, as black, as white, as characterized by western culture, by eastern culture, by every trait that distinguishes one human being from another. Each one of us is in this sense the "Mother of God." Each one of us has given and is giving flesh to the Word of God. When we call Mary the "Mother of God," then, we are celebrating a privilege which is our own. We are also proclaiming a truth about ourselves which we need to reflect upon.

A call to continual conversion

If we really are the body of Christ on earth, and if we are called to let Jesus live and act in everything we do, then the conclusion is obvious: each one of us must keep striving for authenticity. We have to keep trying to become what we are: to become in understanding and desire, in all our words and actions, the embodied presence of Jesus Christ on earth.

This means commitment to spiritual growth. It calls for serious dedication to the goal of total conversion; that is, to complete acceptance of the attitudes and values of the Gospel. If

Jesus Christ is acting with us in all that we do, then it is not enough for us to do our best. We have to do all we can to make our best better. In other words, we have to devote ourselves to lives of *continual change.*

The reality of conversion is change. Conversion is not authentic unless it shows up in our lifestyle: in our choices, our words, our actions, our behavior at home, at work and in our social life. To devote oneself to "continual conversion" can be an illusion. We can hide behind the vagueness of the words. But if we promise God *constant change* we know we have to produce. We can look back and verify whether we have changed anything in our lives since yesterday, the day before, last week or a month ago. Do we speak the same way, dress the same way, drive the same way, vote the same way, spend our time and our money the same way, treat our family, our friends and our business contacts the same way? Do we act as we used to act toward members of minority groups, other races, the poor, the populations of developing countries? Do we speak as we used to speak about social and political issues? A dedication to changing these real things in our lives is a dedication to conversion that is real. And dedication to real conversion is the only way to accept the mystery of our lives, the mystery of being Christ's body, His real presence on earth.

Being the body of Christ on earth gives us something to live up to. It also gives us a new way to think of ourselves. We call Mary the "Mother of God." Can we just as comfortably call ourselves the "body of God" on earth? Can we see ourselves as the *embodied presence of Jesus Christ* in every situation in which we find ourselves? In our social life? In our business and professional (or student) life? In our family environment? In our civic and political involvement? To see ourselves this way is to see ourselves as we are. It is simply to accept the faith. It is to believe in ourselves as the body of Christ the same way we believe in Mary as the Mother of God.

The call to prophetic witness

If we do this, then we should be able to understand more clearly and embrace more seriously our baptismal consecration as *prophets*.

A prophet is anyone who "professes" or expresses the word of God. But in a more precise Christian sense, a prophet is someone who can take the general, abstract teaching of Jesus and apply it to the concrete circumstances of a given time and place. The prophets are always coming up with new and innovative ways to live out the Gospel in family life, in social situations, in business deals and political involvement. And anyone who is conscious of being the body of Christ and is striving in serious ways to be ever more authentically His saving presence on earth in every thought, word and decision, will soon learn what it means to receive, to discern, and to take the risk of following prophetic insights.

A simple way to embrace the call to bear prophetic witness to Jesus on earth is just this: **Resolve that you will never again ask only whether something is right or wrong, but whether it** *bears witness to Jesus Christ.* Your standard of morality from this day forward, your basic question in making ethical decisions, will always be, not, "Is this right or wrong?" but, "Does this bear witness to Jesus Christ? Is this an authentic expression of His teachings, attitudes and values?" You will never ask again,"Do I have to do this?" but always, "Can I bear witness to Christ by doing this?" Never, "Was it wrong for me to say what I just said?" but always, "Did what I say bear witness to the presence of Jesus living and speaking within me?"

If you set out to make every decision in your life, every outward expression of your inner attitudes and values -- in your home, at work, in your social life and in politics -- a visible witness to the truth and priorities of Jesus Christ, then you will **lead a life of continual growth, conversion and change**. And you will be more and more authentically what your baptism made you: the body of Christ, the embodied presence of Jesus Christ on earth.

To be a "prophet" in the Church is to let the words of Christ take flesh in everything we do. To give ourselves in a dedicated way to this is to live out our belief that Mary, through the "Yes" that she spoke to the angel, became the Mother of God; and that we, through the "Yes" we spoke at baptism, became His real body on earth.

REFLECTION AND RESPONSE
to
"MOTHER OF GOD"

SCRIPTURE : *Read:* Luke 1:26-38

PRAYER: Mary, you were asked to surrender your whole life to being the Mother of God. All of your future, all of your plans, you gave up to let yourself be used by God as the instrument of His plan for the renewal of the world.

Mary, pray for me. Guide me through this book so that I will understand what it means for me to be the body of Christ. Pray that I will have the love to embrace my baptismal commitment to be and to live as His body on earth. Pray that I will say yes to all that I have been consecrated to be. And teach me to appreciate what that means. I ask you to pray with me for this to your Son, Jesus Christ our Lord. *Amen.*

OUR OBJECTIVE in this chapter is to understand and appreciate better two things: what it means for Mary to be the "Mother of God," and what it means for us to be the real body of Jesus Christ on earth. Jesus did not take flesh in Mary until she said "Yes" to being the Mother of God. And He cannot act in us as He desires, and renew the world through our human actions, until we say "Yes" with deep understanding and personal commitment to all that our baptism calls us to be. **So the goal of this chapter is a deeper, more informed decision to let Jesus Christ act in me as His own body on earth.**

INVENTORY:
- How do you usually think of yourself in relationship to Jesus? As His friend? Follower, Servant? His body? What word best expresses it?

- Are there any particular things you are doing now to make your life more like the Gospel?
- What particular ways have you discovered to live more authentically the teaching of Jesus?

INPUT:
- What helped me most in this chapter?
- What difference would it make in my life if I began to think of myself always as the body of Christ?

INITIATIVE:
- How can I apply the message of this chapter to my life?
- When, where, and how will I do this?

Note: two things which follow from our being the body of Christ are:
- the call to bear *prophetic witness* on earth by applying the teachings of Jesus in new and creative ways to our own life situations;
- the need for *continual growth and conversion* if we are to be the authentic human presence of Christ.

PRAYER FORM FOR THIS CHAPTER: For ten minutes use the "Prayer of the Five Senses." Take each sense in turn -- sight, hearing, speech and taste, touch, smell -- and compare the way you use these powers with the way Mary or Jesus did. Close with the *Hail Mary*, or any other prayer you like.

MANTRA: *say frequently during the day*: "This is my body, given for you."

CHAPTER TWO
THE VIRGIN BIRTH

Scripture tells us that Mary was still a virgin when Jesus was born (see Matthew 1:25). And this was the first teaching about Mary to be given the precision of a dogmatic formula -- except that the focus of the dogma was not really on Mary at all but on Jesus. In the profession of faith which issued from the Councils of Nicea and Constantinople I (held in the years 325 and 381 A.D.) the Church re-expressed the teaching of Scripture in her own words: "And He (Jesus) was made flesh by the Holy Spirit; and this was from Mary the virgin; and He became a human being." [1]

There are actually four statements here: that Jesus became flesh; that this was by the power of the Holy Spirit; that Mary was a virgin; and that God truly became human. We can reduce these to two if we wish: that God really took human flesh in Jesus, and that this was accomplished, not through the human

---

[1] This is my own, unofficial translation of the Greek text found in Denziger (Enchyridion Symbolorum, No. 86). I have divided it into three parts: "and... and... and" -- following the triple "kai...kai...kai" in Greek.

means of sexual intercourse, but by the power of God acting directly upon Mary. How does this dogma clarify what is said in Scripture, and what does it say that is of practical spiritual value to us today?

From the flesh of a woman

What the dogma makes clear (in response to the various speculations and shocked objections of the time) is that the flesh of Jesus was real flesh, human flesh taken from Mary. It was not just an appearance of flesh -- something prefabricated in heaven so that the divine person of God could come to earth without actually becoming human flesh. Jesus didn't just drop down ready-made from heaven into Mary's womb. He was conceived. Mary's womanly body was used to give God flesh, not just to give Him room.

This means that in Mary the eternal God really began to exist in time and space. In Jesus God actually became part of human life and history on earth. He wasn't just a visitor from eternity who descended into time as in a space capsule, insulated by his divinity from the real conditions of human life on earth. No, He took flesh on earth. He took

flesh of a woman. He became a full participant in fleshed, human existence. This is
what "incarnation" means.

By the power of God

The dogma also repeats the Scriptural teaching that Jesus was conceived by the power of
God acting directly on Mary, without any
human act of sexual intercourse, without any
human father.

It is important for us in our day to take note
of the fact that the only reason why Jesus was
born of a virgin was to make it perfectly clear
that He had no earthly father; that God
Himself was His Father. Our teaching about
the virginity of Mary is in no way -- no way
at all -- a statement about sexuality in general, as if it were a better or more spiritual
thing for a person to remain a virgin than to
marry and engage in sexual intercourse. Or as
if in some way it would have been a defile-
ment for God to have been conceived in an
act of passionate sexual love-making.

We do not teach that Jesus was born of a virgin because it was a better thing to be conceived virginally than through sexual inter-

course. The only reason for the virgin birth was to make it perfectly clear that Jesus was the divine, eternal Son of God the Father, and not just an ordinary human being whom God in some special way adopted and made His own. If Catholics look to the Virgin Mary as to a model of sexual purity, and if we find in her virginity an encouragement to strive for perfect purity in our own lives, this is perfectly justified --but not because of the virgin birth. Mary was pure just as she was perfectly sinless in other respects. She is a model of kindness and love, of faith and prayer, and of every other virtue. And she is a model of purity because she was pure, not because she was a virgin. God did not call Mary to be a virgin in order to say something about sexuality. He called her to be a virgin in order to say something about Jesus, and that is the only reason for the virgin birth.

It is true that, because Mary was a virgin, she is an inspiration and an encouragement to all those who, for one reason or another, must abstain from sexual intercourse -- whether this is because they are not married or because sickness, separation, or some other reason makes intercourse within marriage impossible. Mary's perfect purity within virginity is a sign that sexual abstinence is possible: that it is possible to be perfectly pure -- and happy -- even within a life that is temporarily or even permanently celibate. But it is not her virginity as such which makes Mary a sign and an encouragement for our purity. It is the fact that she was able to be perfectly pure, even though she lived her whole life in the physical abstinence of virginity .

Jesus made flesh in us -- and of us

Mary was a virgin in order that the Word of God might be conceived in her, of her own flesh. But we too, like Mary, have given flesh to the Word of God. We gave our bodies to be the body of Christ. Jesus lives in us. In us God is living and acting in human flesh again, in time and space. In us and through us Jesus Christ is still a part of human life and history. He is present and active in the world -- humanly, in the flesh.

At the Last Supper Jesus promised -- we have to read it twice to make sure He really said it -- "Anyone who has faith in me will do the works I do -- and far greater works than these" (see John 14:12). When we read these words it makes us take seriously the fact that we are the real body of Christ on earth. In each one of us today Jesus can do things that He could not have done in the humanity He was born with, in the body He received from Mary.

For example, Jesus of Nazareth was probably not a genius as we measure human genius. The fact He was divine did not mean He had the highest IQ in the world. It is doubtful that with His human intellect and skills, and especially with His scanty education, Jesus could have given the world the philosophical writings of Thomas Aquinas. He probably could not have expressed His experience of the Father in poetry as beautiful as that of St. John of the Cross. And He would not have been able to help an alcoholic the way another alcoholic can -- the way, as Alcoholics Anonymous has shown us, only another alcoholic can. Jesus could not have painted His own mother's picture or sculpted her in marble as beautifully as Michelangelo did. Jesus was a real human being: in His humanity He was limited. Divine or not, He could not have been the fastest runner and the strongest weightlifter in the world, because these two specializations require two different kinds of bodily development. Each excludes the other.

Obviously it would have been possible for God to work a miracle and make the body of Jesus do any action He chose. God could make a 380 pound Sumo wrestler the winner in a hundred-yard dash! But if God did this, running the race would not be an action *of* the wrestler's body, but an action of God *in* him, propelling him by miracle at a speed incompatible with his weight and size.

One consequence of God's choice to be conceived *of* the virgin Mary, and not just *in* her, is that whenever Jesus acted, what He did was always an action *of* His own humanity, even when He acted divinely. For example, when Jesus taught He expressed divine truth in the language of His own humanity; that is, only in the words that He as a Jew of His times was capable of using, and only through thoughts that could be conceived in His own human consciousness as formed by his life experience, His study and reflection enlightened by the inspirations of God. But it had to be His experience that was enlightened, His study and reflection that was inspired. And so in the teaching of Jesus the truth of God was made flesh in the concepts, the thoughts, the words and images of a first-century Jew who grew up in the country and

34

spoke of farmers sowing seed and women keeping oil in their lamps and little children playing games in the street.

Jesus could not have spoken humanly of the atom bomb, because that would have been impossible to a first-century Jew. And if God had spoken of the atom bomb through Jesus, those words would have been put into His intellect as something prefabricated, ready-made, in heaven; they would not have been words of His human intellect, even of His human intellect united to His divinity. They would have been words of God *placed in* His intellect but not *conceived of* it.

All of this means that Jesus was also limited in what divine actions He could perform through His humanity. He was limited in the ministries He could perform. His divine power acting humanly, acting through His own, particular human nature, would not have been able to accomplish then some of the things it can accomplish now when we let it act in and through our human natures. Jesus acting in us can do some things that would have been impossible to Him acting in the body He was born with. Jesus can do in us some things that are "far greater" than some of the things He did on earth.

This means that what the doctrine of Mary's virginity says about Jesus made flesh in Mary it also says about Jesus made flesh in us: that He really takes to Himself and uses our flesh, the body that is particular and special to each one of us. And when we say Jesus acts through our "bodies," we include in this our minds and our wills, our human understanding and choices. Jesus acts in human flesh on earth only in, through, and in dependence on our human acts. If we do not develop our minds as disciples of Jesus; if we do not read the Scriptures and reflect on them; then in our intellects there will not be the background words and images, the humanly-acquired thoughts or knowledge that God can use to enlighten and inspire us or to instruct others through us.

The doctrine of the virgin birth says to us, then, that whatever we do as the body of Christ on earth, we are going to do with our own humanities. God will only do *in* us what He can do *through* us and *with* us, using the minds and wills, the personalities and bodies we actually have. The humanities we offer to Him to be transformed and given as the bread of life for the world are not only His gift to us, but they are also "the work of human hands" -- the product of our own life experience, reflection and choices.

"By the power of the Holy Spirit" -- in us

At the same time, the doctrine of the virgin birth emphasizes that what we are able to do as Christ's body on earth we do only by the divine power of God. Mary's virginity was a necessary sign of and preparation for her role as Mother of God. She was called to be a virgin in order to make it clear that she was the mother, not just of an ordinary man, but of the Son of God. Her visible human virginity was the sign of her invisible divine motherhood. The fact that she conceived without human means is the sign that she conceived by the power of God. And in this she is a sign to us of our own radical dependence on God and on our union with Him in grace in order to bear fruit or to do anything that is divinely lifegiving on earth. Although in us Jesus acts today in dependence on our human natures; nevertheless, what He does, and what we are able to accomplish acting as His body on earth, is entirely dependent on His presence and power within us. As He said at the Last Supper, "I am the vine, you are the branches....apart from me you can do nothing" (see John 15:5)

Here we have applied to us the two statements included in the Church's dogma about the virgin birth: that God really took human flesh from Mary and that this was accomplished, not through the human means of sexual intercourse, but by the power of God acting directly upon Mary. In us who are His true body on earth, Jesus Christ really lives and acts humanly today, in the flesh. And all that we accomplish as His body, all that we contribute to the salvation of the world, all that we do which gives life, His life, to the world, we do by the power of God acting through us. Not by human means alone, but by the power of God acting in and through our human actions.

Absence of human, sign of divine

Mary's virginity was a sign that the child she bore was conceived by the power of God. In our own lives and ministry there must also be a sign that what we accomplish is accomplished by the power of God, and not just by human resources. It must constantly be visible in our lives -- visible to ourselves and to others -- that in everything we do or undertake we are relying on God's power, not our own. How do we make this visible?

We do not do it by refusing entirely to use human means. Jesus was not just conceived by the power of the Holy Spirit; He was conceived of the virgin Mary, of her own human flesh. And He was brought forth in labor, the way any human baby is born. So our human natures always have a part in the work God does in us. We do not despise what is human. We do not reject it. We do not refuse to use human means.

But we do not rely on the human. And in what we aspire and attempt to do we go far beyond what we could expect to accomplish through the human resources at our disposal. We do not refuse to act until we have sufficient human assurance of success. We do not let the human means available to us determine what goals we will aim at. We muster all the human resources we can, and then attempt to do what they do not suffice for. We find the Scriptural mandate for this expectation of a constant "virgin birth" in our lives in Jesus' instructions to His disciples when He sent them out for the first time to preach. He sent them without the normal provisions for a journey as a sign that they were sent by God (see Matthew 10:7-10). And when He sends us out He likewise tells us not to rely on our academic degrees or our experience or our human qualities, but on the fact we are sent by Him and He is living and working within us. Jesus uses all that we have humanly acquired and developed. But He enlightens us, works in us and makes us bear fruit far beyond what is humanly possible. Because we are sent by Him we base our hopes, not on our human abilities or techniques, but on our conscious, prayerful, self-surrendered union with Jesus our Head who acts in us through His Holy Spirit. We know that any fruit we bear on earth will be brought forth from us by the power of God. And we must make it visible that we know this.

Prayer: of petition and discipleship

Above all, we do this by praying. Prayer is an explicit profession of reliance on God. When married couples pray together every night for God's guidance and help in their marriage, they are showing that they do not rely on their human resources alone. They are expressing dependence on God -- and at the same time revealing that they have embraced an ideal of love and marriage beyond human power to attain. If young people starting a date began it with a prayer it would say they wanted their whole relationship to be on more than an ordinary human level: on a level of interaction, in fact, that is impossible to attain without the active intervention of God. If each one of us were to stop and pray before we start our work each day, that would be a way of saying that we hope to do more through our labor than what appears: that we aspire, in fact, to extend the reign of God on earth through what we do all day.

The true prayer of the virgin mother, however -- of the virgin mother that all of us are called to be -- is the prayer of *discipleship*. This is the prayer that combines the two lessons of the Virgin Birth: a Christian recognition of the human ("conceived of the virgin Mary") with dependence on God ("by the power of the Holy Spirit"). The prayer of discipleship is a serious, prayerful reflection on the word of God, on the message of Jesus. It is an effort to understand and respond to the Gospel by using human neans -- by reading, thinking, and making decisions. But this effort is permeated with awareness that we cannot understand any word of God as we should, or respond to it in any effective way, unless we are enlightened and moved by the Holy Spirit.

It sometimes helps not to use the word "prayer" for the prayer of discipleship. Some people think they can't pray. Others have a particular block against "praying over the Scriptures." They are convinced it won't work for them. So let us not speak of prayer. Let us just ask instead, "Can you read the Scriptures?" If the answer is "Yes, but I don't understand them," then ask, "Can you think about them, reflect on them?" If the answer now is, "Yes, but I don't get any great thoughts; I don't seem to get the insights other people get," then ask the final, practical question: "Can you read something in Scripture and think about it *until* -- "until" is the key word here -- until you think of some way to *respond to it in action?* The action doesn't have to be world-shaking. You don't have to respond with a radical reformation of your whole life. Even a token gesture is enough to make your response to the Scripture real -- just so long as it is some real action in time and space, something concrete that you do.

If you can think about the message of Jesus until it leads you to some real action, some real change in your life -- no matter how small, no matter if it is only for one day, or for the time it takes to do some little thing like smile at a neighbor -- then you are into discipleship. You are making human efforts to understand and to respond to the word of God. In doing this you are showing that you understand both God's need for your developed humanity and your need for enlightenment and help from God.

The prayer of the disciple is the prayer that seeks to understand. It is the prayer that employs all of one's human powers -- memory, intellect and will -- in a continuous, deep, quiet effort to become one with Jesus in mind and will and heart. The disciple *looks* at what Jesus did and *listens* to what Jesus said with burning intent to *understand* all He understands, to *appreciate* everything He values, to *embrace* in choice and action everything He desires. The prayer of discipleship is the prayer we persevere in all our lives, until Jesus is born in us, until in each one of our individual humanities and in the Church as a whole Christ is "brought to full stature" (see Ephesians 4:13).

This prayer goes beyond the prayer of petition, beyond just the expression of dependency on God to accomplish through us what is humanly impossible. It takes seriously the task of preparing our human natures to receive and understand God's inspirations. Discipleship is an effort to develop our human capacity to perceive, to accept and to carry out God's will. The prayer of discipleship is the prayer Mary used when, in response to something her Son did or said -- something she did not understand -- she quietly but actively "treasured all these things and reflected on them in her heart" (see Luke 2:19; and 2: 50-51).

The virgin Mother: image of the Church

To give ourselves to *discipleship* with the goal of disposing our humanities to hear and respond to the words of God is to integrate into our lives the dogma of the Virgin Birth. It is to accept to give flesh to Jesus Christ. It is to surrender ourselves to being His active, living body on earth, continuing His ministry in our time and place and culture. It is to give our flesh for the life of the world -- and to know that we are giving birth to

Christ again, not through human resource-fulness, but by the power of God.

The more we *commit ourselves to living lives characterized by reflection on the words of God,* the more we become able to see in Mary, the virgin Mother of God, the image and sign of what the Church is all about. We see in her the image of what each one of us, as a member of the Church, is all about. And to live out what we see in Mary is to live out what we are.

REFLECTION AND RESPONSE
to
THE VIRGIN BIRTH

SCRIPTURE : *Read:* Matthew 1:18-29.

PRAYER: Mary, you gave birth to the Son of God by the power of God. The Holy Spirit came upon you and the power of the Most High over-shadowed you -- to show us that nothing is impossible with God.

Mary, pray for us that we will believe in what God wants to do through us. Pray that we will let ourselves be taught by God and seek to learn. Pray that we will give ourselves to Him by doing all that we can to understand His word, and that we will bear fruit on earth by believing that the Lord's words to us will be fulfilled. Teach us to be His disciples. We ask you to pray for this to your Son, Jesus our Lord. *Amen.*

OUR OBJECTIVE in this chapter is to understand why Jesus was born of a virgin and to see what it tells us about our own call to give flesh to God in the world.

Briefly, the Virgin Birth teaches us two things: that God really took human flesh of Mary, and that Jesus had no earthly father, but was conceived directly by the power of God. This calls us to do two things: to really *use our human powers and resources* to grow into a more human understanding of the mind of Jesus, while at the same time *relying not on human efforts but on the power of God.* We do this and show our reliance on God **by living lives characterized by discipleship and prayer.**

INVENTORY:
- What are you doing now to be a disciple; that is, to develop your human understanding of Christ's mind? (Be concrete: when, where, how long?)
- What are you doing to make your will more free to respond to His ideals and desires? (In what concrete ways are you working against any tendencies, fears, habits or inertia in yourself which keep you from seeing and accepting His ideals?)
- In what positive, specific ways do you express your awareness of being dependent on God in all that you want to accomplish? Before what actions do you usually say a prayer?

INPUT:
- What helped me most in this chapter?
- What can I do to help make discipleship real for me? How can I develop my human understanding of the message of Jesus?

INITIATIVE:
- How can I apply the message of this chapter to my life?
- When, where, and how will I do this?

PRAYER FORM FOR THIS CHAPTER: Say the rosary, not thinking about the meaning of the individual words, but meditating on the Scriptural story or mystery assigned to each decade.

MANTRA: *say frequently during the day:* "Mary reflected on all these words in her heart."

CHAPTER THREE
THE IMMACULATE CONCEPTION

In 1854 Pope Pius IX defined the dogma of the Immaculate Conception. Many Catholics, and even more non-Catholics, don't have a clear idea of what the doctrine means. This is only because they have not paused long enough to look at the meaning of the words themselves. The words tell us simply that Mary was immaculate at her conception: that she was conceived without coming under the power of sin at all; that from the first moment of Mary's physical existence the sin of the world had no crippling effect on her.

One common misapprehension about the Immaculate Conception is to think it means that Mary herself was conceived without sexual intercourse on the part of her parents, which is false. Other people think the Immaculate Conception means Jesus was conceived in Mary without sexual intercourse -- which is a true fact, but which is the doctrine of the Virgin Birth, not of the Immaculate Conception.

Both of these mistakes are based on the prejudice, common enough in our world, that in some way sexual intercouse is a soiled or "less spiritual" act. Hence, to be conceived without intercourse is to be "immaculately" conceived. To be "conceived without sin" is to be conceived without the passion, the physical pleasure and abandon which some of the early Church writers found so upsetting and unacceptable in intercourse. One of them even offered the opinion that if God had been able to find a way to propagate the human race without the disgusting act of intercourse, He would have done it. Obviously, anyone who has any kind of prejudice against sex, conscious or unconscious, could fall into the error of assuming that what was "immaculate" about Mary's conception was its freedom from sexual involvement.

I mention this prejudice and these misconceptions only to make it clear, as we did with the preceding doctrine of the Virgin Birth, that the Immaculate Conception of Mary has nothing whatsoever to do with sexuality, and "conceived without sin" does not mean in any way "conceived without there being any sin in the act by which she was conceived."

The Immaculate Conception simply states that from the moment of her own conception in her mother's womb, Mary's being was never under the domination of Original Sin. The Immaculate Conception means that Mary herself was "immaculate" at her conception, not that her conception itself was different from any other.

What is Original Sin?

Most people think they understand, more or less, what "Original Sin" is. But the Church herself -- whether we mean by this the Church as a whole or those who teach in the name of the whole Church -- is not too clear about what Original Sin really is. It remains something of a mystery in its details. What we can say about it, drawing on the Church's official doctrine, is this:

- Original sin in us is the effect of the "original" or first sin committed within the human race.

- Because of Original Sin we are born without that special sharing in the life of God which is called "grace," and which now comes to us through baptism. Grace is something that cannot simply be identified with human life as such. It does not belong to human nature as such. It is the gift of participating or sharing in the life which is proper to God alone: divine life, "supernatural" life.

- Original sin does not imply any personal guilt on our part. We are not born "bad" or in any way displeasing to God. What the doctrine does say is that neither the human race as a whole nor any individual in it has the right to blame God for the sorry state of the world or for the effect the environment has on us. The world as we find it is not the world as God created it. Human beings have made it what it is. And for us to complain about what the world does to us is to dissasociate ourselves from the human race. Because we are humans -- because of our solidarity with the human race and with every member of it who has ever sinned -- we are deprived of a gift (grace) which God intended us to have and of the kind of environment God wanted us to grow up in and live in. The doctrine of Original Sin tells us the world is what it is because of human actions, and for us to disclaim all responsibility for what human actions have done to the world is to disclaim membership in the human race.

- Original Sin does not make us foul or displeasing in God's eyes. Our human natures are not "corrupt," either in the sense of being ugly, or in the more philosophical sense of being deprived of some part or element needed to make us integrally human. We are born with all the equipment required for one to live a fully human life.

- On the other hand, because of Original Sin we are born with "darkened intellects and weakened wills." We are "wounded" by Original Sin. This woundedness is more than just the deprivation of grace. We are not just born without divine life; in some way we are wounded in our humanity, in our human existence. But we are just wounded; no part or element is missing that is required for full human functioning.

- This woundedness -- and everything that belongs to Original Sin -- is ours from the very moment, and by the very fact, of our beginning to exist in human flesh, as members of the human race. That is, it characterizes our existence from the instant we are conceived; it is simultaneous with the beginning of our enfleshed, embodied existence.

- Because of this woundedness, and because of the effect human sins have had on the human race, we are all born in some way under the "domination" or power of sin. We have free wills and the freedom to choose, but we are not perfectly free. Evil has a power over us that God did not intend it to have. St. Paul speaks eloquently of this in chapters six to eight of his letter to the Romans.

Without attempting to clarify the whole doctrine of Original Sin or to explain everything the Church teaches about this mystery, I would like to focus on one particular, clear way in which Original Sin wounds us all. Because of the millions of years of human sin -- of individual, free human actions -- the human environment of this world (society) is not what it should be. We are all born into cultures flawed by some distorted attitudes and values, some false priorities, some destructive patterns of behavior -- which we inherit. Every one of us is born into an environment which begins, not only to affect, but to *infect* our feelings, attitudes, choices and behavior from the instant we are conceived. It is impossible for us to grow up in any human culture or society without absorbing some of the prejudices, the distorted attitudes and false values of that society. As a result, our intellects are verifiably distorted and our wills are only too obviously weakened -- subject to pressures and fears, compulsions and paralyzing self-centeredness that cripple our capacity to love.

This woundedness is not something we are personally guilty of: our attitudes and values are to a large part formed before we are old enough or free enough to be guilty of anything. And even as adults we are largely unconscious of the cultural programming that conditions our judgments and decisions. We act on assumptions we are not even aware of, and follow patterns of behavior we have never consciously embraced. But recognized or not, our cultural conditioning does its damage, regardless of how morally innocent or responsible we are. This is a visible, verifiable, experiential woundedness in us all that results from the sin of the world. And this is mostly what I have in mind in the following pages when I speak of Original Sin.

The reason for Mary's exemption

Mary was exempted from this. From the first moment of her enfleshed, human existence, she interacted with her environment the way any other human being does; but she was preserved from any diminishing, enslaving, or crippling effect in her of the sin of the world. Her body, her mind, her humanity were never under the power of sin in any way.

The reason for this was that Mary was destined to be the mother of Jesus the Savior, the Mother of God. And it was not right that the flesh of Jesus, the flesh He took from His mother, should ever have been under the power of sin at any moment. Jesus came to overcome the world; it was not right that He should have been born a slave to it. For this reason the flesh Jesus was to receive from His mother was preserved free from Original Sin from the very first moment of its existence in Mary herself. The doctrine of the Immaculate Conception is no more focused on Mary than any other doctrine about Mary is; like everything else the Church says about Mary, this doctrine is a teaching about Jesus and about His work of redemption as it is realized in us. The Church teaches nothing about Mary except to clarify our understanding of the mystery of Jesus and of our own graced existence as His body on earth, His Church.

What does the doctrine of the Immaculate Conception say about Jesus? What does it say about us?

In a nutshell this doctrine says that *the body of Jesus Christ can never be under the power of sin*. And therefore Jesus today has the power to purify His body from all sin absolutely. We are talking now about Christ's actual body on earth, His sinful body, His Church. This is the body that includes us, the body into which we, with all of our sins and sinfulness, were incorporated at baptism. We will be "immaculately conceived." By the time we enter heaven, by the time Jesus has finished the process of purifying His bride and preparing her for the nuptials of the lamb (see Ephesians 5:25-32 and Revelation 19: 6-8), every one of us will be as absolutely pure of sin as Mary was at her Immaculate Conception. [1]

---

[1] On this see Karl Rahner, S.J., in *Theological Investigations III*.

The power of Jesus over sin

The above may call for some explanation.
First of all, it seems obvious enough that it
would have been inappropriate for the flesh
of Jesus -- the flesh He received from His
mother -- to have been under the power or
domination of sin at any time, in any degree.
It is understandable, therefore, that God
would have preserved Mary from all effects
of sin from the very moment of her conception. [1]

But once Jesus was born and had begun His
work of redeeming the world, He took sin
into His body. As St. Paul rather shockingly
puts it, He was made to "be sin" for our sakes
-- and he adds, even more shockingly, "that
we might become the very holiness of God"
(see 2 Corinthians 5:21). When you and I
were baptized "into Christ" we became

---

[1] Those inclined to be super-logical may argue that the
flesh Mary received from her parents was subject to
Original Sin, so Jesus, by taking human flesh at all,
took flesh that at least remotely had been under the
power of sin. The answer to this is that God does not
push logic beyond the bounds of common sense. Humanly
speaking, it was enough that the flesh Jesus took from
His mother had never been subject to sin; and when God
speaks to us He is always "humanly speaking".

members of His body. We became His body, and our sins -- all the sins we ever had committed or ever would commit -- became the sins of His own flesh. Jesus who was without sin of Himself was "made sin" when He became one with us.

In His identification with us, however, Jesus did not come under the power of sin. Rather, sin came under His power, for He took sin into Himself, not to be dominated by it, but in order to destroy it, so that we might become the "holiness of God." He destroyed sin most radically -- the sins of His own flesh, the sins of His body -- by letting His body be taken to the cross. He died and the sins of the world died in Him. They were annihilated in His death. Then Jesus rose from the dead, but the sins that had died in Him were not raised up with Him. They were left behind in the oblivion of nothingness, of total annihilation.

All of our sins, each and every one of our guilty human acts, were left behind in total annihilation when Jesus died and rose from the dead. We truly died in Christ. But our bodies did not. So while our human, personal history ended, -- died and was renewed -- in the death of Christ, the physical effects of sin in us and in the world did not.We still have physical memories of all that has been programmed into us through our senses, physical addictions and compulsions formed by habits.

And so the corrupting influence of the world -- of the human environment created by centuries of bad human choices -- was not destroyed. Its power was broken but not destroyed. The environment still affects us. The culture still conditions us. The distorted attitudes and values of our society still infect us. The guilt of our personal, human choices, our sins, is taken away when we are baptized and when we repent of sin. But the darkness programmed into our intellects and the weakness that cripples our wills are still a characteristic of human life on earth. The power of sin is still physically present in the world, and everyone physically born into this world is born subject to it.

When we are baptized we are brought "out of the darkness and into His wonderful light" (see 1 Peter 2:9). But all our attitudes and values are not instantly replaced. The light of Christ poured out in our hearts begins gradually to clarify our darkness. His love begins, little by little, to replace the self-centeredness, the ambitions and fears aroused in us by our culture. The infection programmed into us by innumerable human actions born of darkness and death -- our own sins and those of others -- has to be healed by innumerable human actions guided by the light and love of Jesus. This takes time.

The power of darkness has been overcome, and the light has dawned on earth. But everything human is not yet enlightened. The whole mass of dough is not yet leavened, even within each individual member of the body of Christ. The world is redeemed and still being redeemed. Salvation is an accomplished fact and at the same time an ongoing process.

Christian life: Jesus purifying His body

This process is the key to Christian life on earth. In every member of Christ's body who walks the earth sin is present, and the power of sin is at work. But the power sin has over the human race has been radically broken, broken off at the root. And we who are still subject to the power of sin in us and in our environment are gradually being purified, gradually being freed. Nevertheless, in the time and space of this world it is true to say that the body of Christ is infected by sin and still struggling to throw off its distorting, weakening influence.

And so the flesh of Jesus, exempted from all domination of sin from the moment it began to exist in His mother, has now become the carrier of the sins of the world. On earth Jesus was known to be the "friend of sinners" because He sought out their company (see Matthew 9:9-13; Luke 7:34-50 and 15: 1-32; see also Matthew 21:14). We know now that this was just a preview and hint of the union He really sought; that He wanted to do more than just associate with sinners: He wanted to become one with them and make them one with Himself. He did this -- He identified sinners with Himself in the sharing of one life -- when He took us into His own body at baptism. This is what it means to belong to the body of Christ, to the Church, to the community of believers. Into this community all the sinners of the world are invited. Jesus has sent His disciples out along every highroad and byroad to draw them in (see Matthew 22: 1-10).

This is a reversal of God's way of dealing with sin in the Old Testament. God's instructions then were to keep sin out of the people. If anyone committed serious sin, sin that might infect the whole community, that person was to be removed: to be stoned to death or driven out of Israel. The infection must not be allowed to remain (see Deuteronomy 13:6, 17:7, and *passim* through chapter 24).

Jesus reversed this. His instructions to His disciples were to go out and find all the sinners in the world and bring them into His body, into the Church. With Jesus as head of the body, and with His own divine life animating His Church, sin has no power to corrupt and destroy the people of God. The power of the devil is broken; a stronger than he has bound him and repossessed the house he dwelt in (see Matthew 12:25-29; Luke 11:21-26). Now Jesus invites all the infection in the world into His body. He invites it in to make it His own and heal it. His health, His strength, is sufficient to overcome the infection. Jesus draws all the sickness of the world into His own flesh by making every sinner who is baptized "into Christ" a member of His own body. Within that body all guilt is annihilated by Christ's death on the cross, and all the infection of sin is gradually ovecome by the power of Christ's light and love and life.

Baptized into Christ, into His death

This is what happened to us, to each one of us, at baptism. (And it happens to every person who is reborn in Christ, whether by baptism of water, of "blood," or of "desire"). When we were baptized, we were baptized into the body of Jesus hanging on the cross. We died in Him when He died, and we rose again in Him when He rose.

We rose in Him because He rose to live, not only in the body He received from Mary, but in us. He rose in us. He rose to live again, and to continue to live and act and minister in each and every one of the baptized -- to live in human flesh, on earth today, in us who are the members of His body, until the end of time. And so we live now, not as ourselves alone, but as members of His body on earth, as the body of the living, ministering Jesus, who will continue to work visibly, physically and humanly in His Church from now until He comes again (see Romans 6:3-5; Galatians 2:19-20; 3:26-29).

To understand this better, see time as a circle and the body of Jesus hanging on the cross in the middle of it. The circumference of the circle is the time of this world: human history as it unfolds. But the center of the circle is Jesus. Jesus on the cross is the timeless, eternal center of all human history. The crucifixion of Jesus is the moment in view of which the world was made: the event that made creation a blessing instead of a curse, and therefore made it possible. All time, all history, all human life revolve around the cross of Christ.

Every point along the circumference of a circle is equidistant from the center. In the same way, every moment in history is equidistant from the crucifixion of Jesus. This means that each person who is baptized, no matter when that might be in the timeframe of this world, is baptized into the body that hangs on the cross. When we are baptized "into Christ," our bodies become members of His. We, with all of our sins, become members of the body hanging on the cross. At that moment we die in Him, we die His death on the cross, and our sins are annihilated. And each time we repent of new sins committed after our baptism, those sins too are incorporated into His death and simply cease to be. In other words, through baptism Jesus takes into His flesh all of us, with all of our sins, and through His death annihilates our sins. Then, through the power of His risen life in us He continues to purify His body of all the infection worked in us by the sin of the world.

What we have here is the same truth that is proclaimed by the doctrine of the Immaculate Conception: that sin has no power over the flesh of Jesus Christ. Sin cannot have power over Him or His flesh. And since He has made us His flesh and taken us into His body with all of our sins, He has power to purify us from all sin -- not just partially; not just "adequately", but entirely.

From here to eternity: switchbacks

The timeframe can confuse us here. Actually, we are dealing with two different time-frames: time as God sees it from heaven, and time as we experience it here on earth.

To God, seeing things from the viewpoint of His own eternal fullness of being, certain things are already an accomplished fact which to us are still in the process of becoming. For example, from the viewpoint of eternity, Jesus overcame sin and death once and for all on Calvary, when He died on the cross. He redeemed the whole human race in that one act. But from our perspective here on earth, individuals are redeemed or "saved" as each one accepts the grace of Christ and is baptized into His death. From this persepective the redemption of the human race is still going on, and will go on until the end of time.

Christ's body still struggling in this world

If we apply these two different timeframes to the question, "Is the body of Christ under the domination of sin now?" the answer will depend on the timeframe we are using. From the viewpoint of this earth, where things are still happening and the work of establishing the Kingdom is still going on, yes, there is a sense in which the body of Christ is still in some degree subject to sin. St. Paul is our witness again, as he cries out in his letter to the Romans: "I see in my body's members another law at war with the law of my mind; this makes me a prisoner of the law of sin in my members. What a wretched man I am! Who can free me from this body under the power of death?" And later: "We ourselves, although we have the Spirit as first fruits, groan inwardly while we await the redemption of our bodies" (Romans 7:23-24; 8:23).

Within the timeframe of this earth Jesus is still at work in His Church, redeeming all that is human, establishing the Kingdom, bringing all things in heaven and on earth together under His headship (see Ephesians 1:10). He is working through His members to "build up the body of Christ, till we become one in faith and in the knowledge of God's Son, and form that perfect man who is Christ come to full stature" (Ephesians 4:12-13).

In this timeframe Jesus is still purifying His bride, until He can "present to Himself a glorious church, holy and immaculate, without stain or wrinkle or anything of that sort" (Ephesians 5: 25-27).

Jesus is victorious

On the other hand, God already sees the triumph of Christ as an accomplished fact. From the viewpoint of eternity, everyone who would ever be incorporated into Christ through baptism was already present "in Him," in His body, when He hung on the cross. We all died in Him and rose in Him, and all our sins were annihilated forever -- including those we haven't committed yet! In Christ who died and has risen, the Father sees us, not just in our present state of imperfection as we grow toward the fullness of surrender to Christ in love, but already as the bride prepared for the bridegroom, holy and immaculate, with no imperfection at all.

A challenge to faith

The Immaculate Conception of Mary is a sign of this. Mary was *preserved* from all sin as a sign that we would be *purified* of all sin. Just as it was right that the body, the flesh, the Savior took from His mother should never have been under the domination of sin at any time, it is even more right that the flesh the Savior joined to Himself through baptism should be absolutely and totally delivered from the domination of sin through His power. The Immaculate Conception is a sign of Christ's power over sin -- a power that is not limited. Whether He preserves His flesh from sin or purifies it, the end result is the same: sin can have no domination at all over the flesh of the body of Christ. And it will not.

Do we believe this? The challenge of the Immaculate Conception to our faith is to believe that the power of Jesus over sin is so strong that we ourselves -- and every member of the body of Christ on earth -- actually can be "made perfect" as our heavenly Father is perfect (see Matthew 5:48). We have to believe that Jesus can deliver us *entirely* from the domination of sin, from all that we experience and regret and groan under as our own inability to love purely and passionately and perfectly in response to other people and to the love we receive from God.

The Immaculate Conception is not just something nice that happened to Mary. Nor is it just a comforting promise that one day all of us will be perfectly purified of sin. This doctrine is a challenge to faith. It is a promise that is also a proclamation. And a proclamation is something to be believed -- to be believed and answered in action. The Immaculate Conception comforts us, yes -- but at the same time challenges us and summons us to live as people who believe that absolute purity of heart, the absolute perfection of love, is not only our ideal but our destiny. It is a promise that challenges us to live in unmitigated hope.

What does this mean on the level of everyday life? The key words to our answer will be *environment, Savior* and *interaction.*

Original Sin and the human environment

The first thing we have to do is see how Original Sin appears in our everyday life. In a sense, every sin does what the first or original sin of the human race did: it puts something into the environment that just never goes away. Every sin -- in fact, every human act, good or bad -- makes the environment of this world a little different, and that difference affects other people and influences their behavior.

In a world in which people have been making choices, interacting with each other, and having an effect on the environment for thousands of years, it is impossible to measure how much distortion of truth and falsification of values has taken place. Falsehood is as common as the air we breathe. And every human being's existence is affected by this. Every single person who is born into this world in the flesh -- that is, who has a body with which to interact with the environment -- is subject to the influence of this world's darkness and this world's distorted value system from the very first moment of physical existence. To exist in the flesh is to be subject to the influence of the environment. And since sin is part of the environment, to exist at all is to be subject to sin.

Theoretically, it wouldn't have to be this way. We have minds and wills. We can judge between truth and falsity, good and evil, and we are free. But in actual fact, given the way we learn, the way we make decisions, and the time it takes for us to grow into wise, self-disciplined, spiritually-motivated people, the sin of the world is going to infect all of us -- distorting our attitudes and values, weakening our love, inclining us to selfishness, manipulation and violence -- before we are even old enough to choose for ourselves as adults. In other words, all of us without exception come under the power of sin in this world from the moment we are conceived in our mother's womb.

Jesus the Light and Life of the world

This casts new light on our understanding of Jesus as Savior. He is not just the one who takes away the sins of the world by dying on the cross, so that the way is now open for us to enter heaven. Jesus is also the one who "saves" our existence in this world: saves everything we do from destructiveness and distortion, from meaninglessness and mediocrity, by being the Light and Life of the world. Where the culture has distorted our attitudes, Jesus instructs us with truth -- a truth that the darkness of this world has not in any way diminished. Where the world teaches us the way of self-interest and violence, Jesus teaches -- and shows us by example -- the way of peace and selfless love. In other words, Jesus is an ongoing Savior. Once we have been joined to Him in baptism as participating in His divine life -- in His divine understanding and love -- He little by little overcomes the darkness in us with His light, the selfishness in us with His love. He gradually converts us into total likeness to Himself.

This is what it means to be "saved." It is, like life itself, both an either-or fact and an ongoing process. Just as people are either alive or dead, but can be more or less alive, so people are either reborn in grace and sharers in divine life or they are not -- but if they are, they can enter more or less fully into the divine life and light and love that Jesus shares with them. "Salvation" is sharing in the divine life of Jesus Christ. And we grow into the fullness of salvation as we grow into total likeness to Jesus Christ in mind and will and heart.

Interaction, the key to salvation

The key to salvation, then, is relationship with Jesus Christ. But the reality of any relationship is *interaction*. Our relationship with anyone is only as real as our interaction with that person. The relationship is only as deep as the level of our interaction. And it only includes as much of our life as is affected by our interaction.

So the decision to accept Jesus Christ as Savior -- if it is authentic and complete -- is really *a decision to make Jesus Christ an active part of everything we do for the rest of our lives.* It is a decision based on a positive, lifegiving act of despair and hope: a despair of escaping from the darkness and destructiveness of this world's environment without Him, matched by an absolute confidence in His power to free entirely from the power of sin all those who become sharers in His life and members of His body, and who interact responsively with His mind, His words, His inspirations, His ministering body on earth.

This is a decision to make Jesus Christ an *active part* of our family life, of every social gathering and event, of our business or professional (or student) life, of our civic and political involvement. It is a commitment to interact with Him in the process of making every decision, every choice of our lives from now on.

This is what it really means to accept Jesus as Savior. And this is what it means, most basically, to be a Christian. And this is what the Immaculate Conception of Mary calls us to by being for us a sign and a promise of Jesus Christ's absolute power over all the sin and darkness of the world. The question now is, do you believe in that power enough, and are you sufficiently convinced of your absolute need for it, **to decide in a serious way to make Jesus Christ an active participant in every area and activity of your life from now on?** Do you really believe in Him and accept Him as the Savior that He is? If so, how will you make Him a part of everything you do?

REFLECTION AND RESPONSE
to
THE IMMACULATE CONCEPTION

SCRIPTURE : *Read:* Luke 1:46-55

PRAYER: Mary, all generations will call you blessed and see in you the sign of the power of God. From the first moment of your existence you were preserved from all infection of evil. You came into the darkness of this world with undiminished light. You entered this world of selfishness filled with love. You are the promise of God made flesh: God will deliver us from all sin.

Mary, pray for me that the message of your Immaculate Conception will penetrate to my heart. Pray that I will believe in the power of your Son to purify me of all sin. Pray that this belief will give me hope, and that this hope will motivate me to make your Son a part of everything I do. *Amen.*

OUR OBJECTIVE in this chapter is to believe in the power Jesus has over all the effects of sin in us: whether these come from the sins we have committed or from the infection of our environment. We will be purified.

The expression of our belief in Christ's power to free us from the power of sin at work in our world -- and the expression of our belief that He is the only one who *can* free us -- is best given in the **decision to make Jesus an active part of everything we do**. If we make interaction with Jesus an integral part of our family and social life, our business decisions and political options, then, yes, we can claim to know Him as Savior.

INVENTORY:
- What is it in yourself that you dislike the most? Where did this come from?
- Can you imagine yourself purified, not only of all your sins, but also of everything that you don't like in yourself? Do you believe this will happen?
- In what specific, concrete ways do you interact with Jesus now in your family life? Social life? Business or student life? Civic life?

INPUT:
- What helped me most in this chapter?
- What concrete ways of interacting with Christ would express my real belief in the power of Christ and my real reliance on Him as Savior?

INITIATIVE:
- How can I apply this chapter to my life?
- When, where, and how will I do this?

PRAYER FORM FOR THIS CHAPTER: Find a time and place where you can be quiet for a few minutes, and quietly review the day. Look for moments when you felt less good about yourself, or when, looking back, you do not like what you see. Now try to imagine yourself as different; as perfectly purified of whatever inclinations, habits, desires, or patterns of behavior you have just focused on. Imagine what this would be like. Rest in an act of faith and gratitude that this will be your reality in heaven.

MANTRA: *say frequently during the day*: "O Mary conceived without sin, pray for us who have recourse to you."

CHAPTER FOUR
"EVER VIRGIN" -- "EVER IMMACULATE"

So far we have looked at the doctrine that is central to all devotion to Mary and all theological reflection on her -- the dogma that Mary is the "Mother of God" -- and we have worked backward through two mysteries of Mary's life which were presupposed to or prerequisites for her being made the Mother of God: the Virgin Birth and the Immaculate Conception. The Virgin Birth was required so that it would be clear that Jesus had no father but God Himself. The Immaculate Conception was required so that the flesh of the Savior would never have been under the domination of sin.

Now we are going to move in the opposite direction: to see what mysteries in the life of Mary *follow* from the fact that she was the Mother of God. These fall into two cateegories: the doctrines which speak of the extension in time of the Immaculate Conception and the Virgin Birth (these are the doctrines which say Mary was "ever immaculate" and "ever virgin") and the doctrine of the Assumption. We will begin by asking why Mary's sinlessness and virginity had to be "forever," and in a second chapter extend the teaching on Mary's sinlessness to include the expression "full of grace." Then we will look at the meaning of her Assumption.

Why "ever?"

The teaching of the Church is that Mary was "immaculate" or preserved free from all sin, not only from the first moment of her existence in her mother's womb, but for the whole of her life. The special privilege of the Immaculate Conception was extended, so that Mary was preserved, not only from Original Sin, but from all personal sin, and this for the whole of her life. She never committed any sin, serious or slight, from the moment she was conceived in her mother's womb until she the moment she was joined to her Son in heaven. This is the doctrine that says Mary was "immaculate" for all of her life and "ever sinless." This special grace extends the privilege of the Immaculate Conception in time: Mary was not just preserved from all domination by sin until Jesus could take flesh from her, but even after Jesus was born she was kept totally free of sin, and this until the end of her life.

Why did God grant Mary this special privilege? We have already seen why Mary should have been preserved free of all sin *until* the birth of Jesus: this was so that the flesh of the Savior would never have been under the domination of sin at any time. But after Jesus was born, what difference did it make? Why was it so important for God to preserve her by special privilege free of all sin for the rest of her life? Why "ever" immaculate?

The same extension was given to the virginity of Mary. In teaching that she was "ever virgin," the Church is saying that Mary continued to live as a virgin even after Jesus was born and the fact had been established that He had no earthly father. Why was this? Why should Mary not have borne children by St. Joseph after Jesus? Why did God call her to be "ever" virgin? We have seen why both sinlessness and virginity were required of Mary *prior* to the birth of Jesus. But what is the connection between being "Mother of

God" and remaining sinless and virgin after that? [1]

That Mary was "ever virgin" was definitely taught by the Second Council of Constantinople in the year 553. No reason for this is included in the official proclamation, and we can hardly accept -- at least, on face value -- the one given earlier by Pope Siricius in a letter written to the bishop of Thessalonica in 392. Siricius' argument was that Jesus would hardly have chosen to be born of a virgin if He thought she would be so incontinent later that she would defile with seed from human intercourse the womb in which the body of the Lord had been conceived! (In Denzinger, *Enchiridion Symbolorum*, no. 91).

We spontaneously interpret this argument as if it were based on the biased assumption that human intercourse is somehow defiling, or at least unworthy of flesh as holy as Mary's.

---

[1] It is important to keep in mind that the connection is *not* between being "ever virgin" and "ever sinless." The Church is making no identification of virginity with sinlessness. These are taken together because they both extend in time the mysteries they are rooted in: the Virgin Birth and the Immaculate Conception.

And that may have been Siricius' personal attitude, or it may not have been; only historians could say. But that assumption does not necessarily underlie Siricius' argument.

Not just to do , but to be

We have seen that the only reason for the virgin birth was to make it clear that Jesus had no earthly father. For this reason the virginity of Mary is a sign that Jesus was the Son of God. Mary was called to be virgin because she was called to be Mother of God.

But the title "Mother of God" does not just speak of something Mary *did*; it speaks of what she *is*. Mary was not just "used" once to be the mother of Jesus and then forgotten, as if she had signed up for it on a contract basis. No, it is very important for us to recognize that through her selection by God to give birth to the Savior she *became* the "Mother of God." She was consecrated to *be* what she was called to do. Her "Let it be done unto me according to your word" was not just consent to render a service, to loan herself to God for the act of giving birth to the Savior. It was the surrender of her whole life, her whole being to God. Like baptism, marriage or ordination, it was an act which altered her relationship to God and to every other human being on earth forever.

The call to give birth to the Savior made Mary different forever. Henceforth she would be the "Mother of God." That would be her reality. As such, she could never be the mother of ordinary human beings in the ordinary way. She would be the mother of the whole human race, it is true: the mother of all the redeemed. But she would be this by being the mother of the redeemer. Once she accepted to be the Mother of God, every relationship she would ever have with any other person would pass through this, her relationship with Jesus. She is what she is for us because she is the Mother of God. And the sign of what she is continues to be the sign that pointed in the first place to her divine motherhood: her virginity. Mary is "ever virgin" because she is "ever Mother of God." And she is ever Mother of God because the act by which she became Mother of God was not just a service she was called to render. It was not an action like any other. It was an act which consecrated her to a special, a unique relationship with God forever. The visible sign of that consecration must remain as long as the consecration remains; that is, forever.

And that is the real, the valid point of Pope Siricius' argument: it was unthinkable that someone chosen to be what Mary was chosen to be -- the Mother of God -- could ever be mother in any way that did not follow from this. Nor could she accept any other seed of life within herself after accepting the Word of God.

Joseph's choice

St. Joseph knew this. One interpretation of his decision to "divorce her quietly" when he learned Mary was pregnant is that Joseph had no doubts about Mary's virtue at all; he just reacted as any devout Jew would have reacted when it became clear to him that his fiancée had been chosen to be the mother of God's own Son. Joseph excused himself and began to back out of the picture. Obviously he could not continue with his plans to marry Mary if God had chosen her for Himself. It was only when God told him explicitly not to fear, but to take Mary as his wife, that he dared to go ahead with the wedding (see Matthew 2:18- 25).

"Dared" may not be the best word. "Accepted" might be better. Joseph knew that the marriage he had expected to have with Mary would never be. She could never be just his wife in the way other men's wives were theirs. God had chosen her to be the mother of His Son. And that Son was not to be conceived through a human act of sexual intercourse as other children of promise had been: Isaac, for example, and John the Baptizer (see Genesis 17:15-22 and 21:1-8; Luke 1:13-25). Joseph was not being asked to have a son by Mary whom God would consecrate for a special destiny. God had chosen Mary as no other woman in history had ever been chosen, to bear the Son of God Himself. Joseph knew this made their relationship different forever. After the angel clarified things for him, he did not so much "dare" to take her as accept to take her as a wife with whom he would live in virginity forever. Joseph surrendered all the hopes and dreams he had had of complete physical union with the girl he loved. He too said "let it be done according to your word," and the world has never given him sufficient credit for it.

Extension of the Immaculate Conception

The same reasoning explains why Mary was "ever immaculate," ever sinless. She was not just exempted from Original Sin in order to be used to give flesh to the Son of God -- used and then cast aside. She was preserved from all domination of sin in order to be the Mother of God. And just as she was consecrated *for* this role by sinlessness beforehand, so she was consecrated *by* it to a sinlessness that would be forever.

Mary's Immaculate Conception is a sign of hope for us, standing as a promise that we who became the flesh of Christ by baptism will also be "immaculately conceived" -- that the flesh of Christ which we are will one day be delivered completely from all the power of sin. In the same way the fact that she was "ever sinless" is a sign and a proof that our baptism was not just an isolated act but the beginning of a process. God's power is able to see through to the end what He initiates. Baptism didn't just cleanse us; it recreated us, gave us new life. By baptism we became the body of Christ. And sin cannot have power over the body of Christ. So God's power must bring our identity to its logical conclusion. The continuing sinlessness of Mary, who was never under the domination of sin, is an encouragement to us who still experience that domination to keep hoping and striving for total deliverance, total surrender, total union with Christ our head. The Immaculate Conception of her who was to give flesh to God by childbirth is the pledge of an "immaculate conclusion" for us who became the flesh of Christ by baptism. And Mary Immaculate, Mary "ever sinless," is a sign and a promise that our baptism is still at work in us.

This means Mary's perfect sinlessness is for us an encouragement and a call. Mary, who at her Immaculate Conception was preserved from Original Sin, was preserved from all sin for the whole of her life because she was the Mother of God. We who by baptism were emancipated from the power of this world and delivered from sin in order to become the body of Christ on earth, are now consecrated to a life of total sinlessness because we are His body. Mary's continued sinlessness is a sign to us that our baptism was not just an act that "saved" us, but an act that consecrated us.

At baptism we were not just washed or plunged into the water; we were also anointed with chrism (the word from which "Christ" comes, meaning the "Messiah" or "Anointed One"). We were anointed to be Christ's body, His saving presence on earth.

We were anointed and consecrated to share in Christ's saving mission as *Prophet*, *Priest* and *King*. Our baptism, then, is not just something we are grateful for, but something we must be faithful to. By baptism we are not just redeemed but consecrated. We are not just washed but anointed; not just saved but sent. We are consecrated to be and to act as the body of Christ upon earth.

This leads us to a new image of ourselves. We are not just ordinary people, and we don't relate to others -- or to God -- in an ordinary way. We are the body of Christ -- for God and for others -- wherever we go, whatever we do. Being the flesh of God upon earth, being the embodied presence of Jesus Christ in the world, makes everything different for us.

Being conscious of what we are

Married people wear wedding rings. It reminds them of their consecration to one another and declares the terms of the relationship anyone else can expect to have with them. Priests dress in a way that declares what they are and lets people know what to expect in relationship with them. But every

Christian is, in fact, espoused to Jesus Christ in a relationship as real as that which Mary had with God as the mother of His Son. And every Christian has said to Jesus Christ in baptism, "This is my body, given up for you," in a gift as real as that which husbands and wives make to one another in matrimony. Every one of us is, in fact, the body of Christ: surrendered to Him, consecrated by Him, dwelt in by Him, inspired by Him, empowered by Him as we **go out every day to be His lifegiving, loving presence to everyone we meet**. To consciously accept this image of ourselves -- which is our true reality -- and to commit ourselves to expressing it in everything we do, this can be a major act of conversion in our lives. It is the conversion to which this chapter invites us.

We love "Mary Immaculate," not because she is the model of all virtues, some paragon of perfection standing on a pedestal above and apart from us all. We don't even love her primarily because of all the things she prays for in the world -- such as world peace, precious as this is. We love Mary most of all just because of what she *is*. And what she is tells us what we are called to be.

Mary is our mother. She is our mother because she is the Mother of God, the mother of Jesus. To accept her as our real mother is to accept ourselves as the real body of Christ. To accept her as our Immaculate Mother is to accept ourselves as called -- and encouraged -- to be immaculate.

Mary was the one person most intimately united with Jesus in His act of taking flesh to save the human race. She was the chosen instrument of His incarnation. Because it was through her that He became one of us, Mary was, is and remains associated most intimately with Him in all that He came to do. She is united with Him in His work of giving life to the world. She cares for everything He cares for, and therefore cares most tenderly for us. She is our mother and she loves us like a mother. She cares for us like a mother.

But we too are united with Jesus in everything He came to do. We are His body on earth, the continuation of His saving, redeeming presence. He has taken flesh in us, and through us continues to give life to the world. Therefore we, like Mary, must care for all He cares for, love every person He loves, and give ourselves for the life of every single individual by letting Jesus within us give Himself to others through every word and action of our lives.

There are many different attitudes we can adopt as we go out to meet the world each day. We can be "managers," alert to see what is or is not meeting our expectations from moment to moment. We can be "performers," looking for attention and applause. We can be "gunslingers," ready to overcome or to be overcome in every encounter of the day. We can be "cardplayers," constantly seeking to gain something as we play out each hand. The list could be extended. Or we can go out each day to meet the world simply as the lifegiving body of Christ, seeking above all things to love and give life to every person we meet.

To do this is to live out the grace of our baptism as Mary lived out the grace that made her the Mother of God. And this, more than any other thing, will lead us to be "ever sinless" and "ever virgin" in the sense of being always the singlehearted instruments of God's lifegiving action on earth.

REFLECTION AND RESPONSE
to
"EVER"

SCRIPTURE : *Read:* John 13: 34-35

PRAYER: Mary, you are our mother. In every need we turn to you and you care for us. Yours is a love we can count on. Knowing you and knowing your love makes life different for us here on earth.

Mary, I would like to be loving in the same way you are for everyone I deal with. I am the body of Christ for the world, His embodied presence on earth. Pray for me that I might surrender myself to God and for others as completely as you did. I offer my body, and all my embodied actions, for the life of the world. Ask your Son to live and love in me without reserves. I ask you to pray with me for this to Christ our Lord. *Amen.*

OUR OBJECTIVE in this chapter is to adopt a new image of ourselves -- **to see ourselves as the body of Christ, living to give life to others through love**.

The grace given to Mary is the image of what we are called to be. We are the body of Christ, joined to Him in His lifegiving work. Therefore we are called to be in every action and choice what in fact we are: the body of Christ on earth bringing His divine life to every person through love. The choice to try to do this every day -- is the objective proposed in this chapter.

INVENTORY:
- What is your habitual, your ordinary attitude each day toward the people you deal with?
- What images do you have of yourself which affect your relationship with the people you deal with?

- How does your relationship with Christ affect your relationships with other people?

INPUT:
- What helped me most in this chapter?
- How can I best live out in my dealings with others the identity I have as the body of Christ on earth?

INITIATIVE:
- How can I live out this chapter in my life?
- When, where, and how will I do this?

PRAYER FORM FOR THIS CHAPTER: Spend some time just prayerfully repeating to yourself, "I am the body of Christ...my flesh for the life of the world." Say this over and over, absorbing its meaning and value, for as long as you desire. Then try to repeat it frequently -- even constantly -- to yourself during the day as you go about your ordinary business.

MANTRA: *say frequently during the day*: "I am the body of Christ -- my flesh for the life of the world!"

CHAPTER FIVE
"FULL OF GRACE"

In this chapter I am going to go beyond the Church's precise, dogmatic teaching about Mary's sinlessness and assume that she was also "full of grace."

Mary is called "full of grace" constantly in Catholic tradition, of course. The words of the *Hail Mary* have been prayed for centuries, and they address her precisely as "full of grace." The Scripture scholars say, however, that the Greek word *kekcharitomene* (see Luke 1:28), which we have traditionally translated "full of grace," would actually be better translated as "highly favored daughter." And so we cannot claim this Scriptural word as sufficient proof in itself that Mary was in fact full of grace according to the meaning these words have for us and according to the particular explanation I will give of them. I believe, however, that the explanation I am going to give follows, first of all, from the Church's doctrine on Mary's sinlessness, and that, secondly, it is a faithful clarification of traditional belief and teaching about Mary in the Church. [1]

"Blessed among women"

Pope John Paul II, in his encyclical *Mother of the Redeemer*, explains the expression "full of grace" by relating it to the "blessing" Paul proclaims as the goal and fruit of our redemption: "Blessed be the God and Father of our Lord Jesus Christ, who has bestowed on us in Christ every spiritual blessing in the heavens."

And what is this blessing? It is:

> *to be holy and immaculate in His sight;*
> *to be full of love;*
> *to be His adopted sons*
> (see Ephesians 1:3-6).

---

[1] Pope John Paul II, in the encyclical he wrote for the Marian Year, 1987, gives some sixteen references to the way the expression "full of grace" was interpreted throughout Christian tradition, from Origin and St. John Chrysostom through St. Jerome and St. Bernard. And I have drawn for my explanation from the one he himself gives in his encyclical. See *Mother of the Redeemer*, Part I, Chapter One, note 21 in the Daughters of St. Paul edition, Boston, 1987.

The "blessing" is simply grace: the favor of sharing in God's own life by being incorporated into the body of Christ, with everything this entails. As members of Christ we are all *filii in Filio*, "sons in the Son." In Him, because we are His body, we died with Him on the cross and rose with Him. For this reason we are freed from our sins and able to be "holy and immaculate" in God's eyes, who sees us already as the bride of Christ "holy and immaculate, without stain or wrinkle," ready for the nuptials of the lamb (see Ephesians 5:27).

As Mother of God Mary was joined to Jesus in the work of salvation more intimately than any other person. She gave Him her flesh to be His body. Her consent was required for the Incarnation. It was she who, first among all human beings, had to accept to be the body of Christ: to let Him live in her; to give her flesh to Him and with Him for the life of the world. And therefore it was right that in her should be realized most perfectly, most fully, that "blessing" which Jesus came to give: the blessing of being one flesh with Him, of sharing in His life and mission, of being true children of the Father.

And so Pope John Paul sees in the words with which Elizabeth greeted Mary -- "blessed are you among women" -- more than just a high compliment. They are the proclamation of a unique status. She is blessed as no other woman, no other person is. She has the "blessing" of which St. Paul speaks, the fruit of redemption, in its fullness. If all of us are blessed in Christ, she is "the blessed one," blessed among women, blessed among all the children of God; the one who, during her earthly life, was the most redeemed of all the redeemed.

For this reason, although the Scripture scholars tell us that the word we translate as "full of grace" in the *Hail Mary* probably meant no more in itself than "highly favored daughter" according to the linguistic usage of the time, still we can say that theologically, and in the context of what the angel was actually announcing to Mary, it meant Mary was chosen to be the embodiment of the "blessing" of grace in its fullness.

The meaning of "full of grace"

So I take the words "full of grace" to mean exactly what they say: that Mary was "fully graced" at every stage of her growth in the greatest measure possible for her at that moment. To make this more clear we have to be precise about what "grace" means.

Grace is not a thing, or some reality that could be created by itself, and "poured into" the soul until it overflows. The soul is not a receptacle. So obviously, when we say, "full of grace," we are talking in images. The word "grace" just means "favor." Grace is the favor, the favor of all favors, that came to us through Jesus Christ. And what is this favor? It is the favor of sharing in God's own life, in the divine life, the eternal life that is proper to God alone.

If grace is the favor of sharing or participating in God's life, then to be "full of grace" means to share or participate in God's life as fully as is possible for someone during this earthly life; or, for any given individual, as fully as one's particular stage of human development allows. An infant, for example, cannot share in God's adult thoughts or desires. And so an infant could be "full of grace"even though unable to share fully in the mind of God. (If the infant died, of course, the obstacle would no longer exist. After death we no longer depend on our bodily development to function. In heaven everyone is fully developed!) And so the true measure of grace in any individual, at any stage of that person's life, is determined by only one thing: *surrender* -- surrender to whatever God, within that person's heart, desires to do.

To say that Mary was "full of grace" is the same thing as saying that she was fully surrendered to God's life and action within her, to His inspirations and movements, to His every will and desire. To say she was full of grace is to say that her humanity was totally surrendered to the God who had joined Himself to her, and her to Him, in grace; that is, in a mutual sharing of His divine life with her and of her human life with Him. God could act in her and through her without any resistance at all from her will.

No visible difference at all

The conclusion from this is a strong statement, but one that logically follows: If Mary was full of grace, fully surrendered to God, then her humanity was just as surrenered to the God who dwelt within her by grace as the humanity of Jesus was surrendered to His own divinity. This means that God was as free to express Himself in and through her human nature, her feminine body and characteristics, as He was to express Himself through the masculine body and characteristics of Jesus. Nothing in the humanity of Jesus and nothing in the humanity of Mary distorted God's self expression at all. He could be in each of them and express Himself in each of them, through everything that each one was and did, without distortion or diminishment.

This is the shocking conclusion. Mary was not God. She was simply a human being graced as we are, But if she had been God; if Mary had been God made flesh as a woman instead of as a man in Jesus, *we wouldn't have seen any difference in her at all.*

It stands to reason. If Mary was full of grace; if she was totally surrendered to God at every moment; if her humanity put up no more resistance to anything God wanted to say or do in her and through her than the humanity of Jesus did to His own self-expression as God, then God was able to express Himself in and through her feminine human nature just as freely as He could have if He had taken flesh as a woman to begin with.

God in Himself is neither male nor female; or better, He is everything that in us takes male and female form. He could just as easily have become flesh as a woman instead of as a man. Then, probably, we would know God today as Mother, Daughter and Holy Spirit. But God had to choose. Human beings are either male or female, and for God to become human meant that He had to be one or the other. For reasons known to Himself alone He chose to take flesh as a male.

But God could not express everything God is through a male human nature alone, anymore than He could express all He is through a female human nature. Humanity itself cannot be adequately expressed through just the one or the other. That may be why God arranged that babies should have two parents to introduce them to human life. And it may be one of the reasons why God called Mary to be full of grace: so that we could see in one woman the feminine characteristics of God expressed humanly without diminishment or distortion, just as in Jesus we can see God's masculine characteristics faithfully expressed. God took flesh in Jesus to show us what God could be as a man and what a man would be like as God. In Mary He shows us what God could be as a woman and what a woman would be like as God.

Our call to be "full of grace"

The conclusions don't stop here, however. God cannot fully express Himself through any one human nature, no matter how perfectly it is united to Himself. God could not show us in Jesus, for example, the beauty of God made flesh as a retarded child. In Jesus God was not embodied in a humanity of African culture, or Chinese, or Scandinavian. And even within any given nationality, culture or category, no one individual could express totally or even adequately all the goodness and beauty of God. God can reveal Himself in you in ways in which it would be impossible for Him to reveal Himself in me, and vice-versa. And so every human being is called to be a particular, a special, a unique manifestation of the goodness and beauty of God made visible in human nature. And we can answer this appeal from God perfectly only by being "full of grace." Only through total surrender.

Mary, then, is a model of what we are called to be. When the Church celebrates Mary as "full of grace," the real focus is not on her at all. What we are looking at is what we are called to be. We see our own call and destiny fulfilled in her, and its realization in her holds up to us the possibility of its realization in us. It activates our faith and arouses our hope. Mary is the sign, the image of perfectly graced humanity, of the gift of grace brought to its fulfillment. When we look at her we know what the goal of our life is: it is to surrender so completely to God dwelling within us by grace that He can express Himself in and through our humanities, our own human natures and personalities, as freely as He expressed Himself in Jesus and in Mary, without diminishment or distortion. When the process of our purification, our surrender to Him is complete, and when our names are finally written on our tombstones (as a proclamation that we have finished creating ourselves as persons, finished writing the meaning of our names by our choices), our friends, ideally, should be able to stand there and say, "Old friend, you weren't God. No one knows better than we do how often you did not act like God. But we have to acknowledge that by the time you died, by the time you finished your course, if you had been God Himself made flesh again, we wouldn't have seen any difference!" This is what it means to be "full of grace," and this is God's invitation to us all.

To surrender the self that I am

That is the challenge of this chapter: to define and understand "perfection" as the total surrender of what I actually am -- here and now -- to what Jesus Christ wants to be in me here and now. To be perfect, to be a "saint," does not mean that I have to become something different, some other kind of person. It means that I surrender my actual being -- my actual body, mind, emotional makeup, my present emotional state, even -- to whatever Jesus Christ wants to express in and through me at this moment. I don't have to be smart to be a saint (the Curé of Ars and St. John Francis Regis were just plain dumb -- and Regis was a Jesuit!). I don't have to be likeable (St. Joseph Cupertino's own mother didn't like him!). I don't have to be emotionally well-balanced or have a naturally sweet disposition. There have been impatient saints and choleric saints; saints who were constantly filled with sexual desires of every possible kind, and saints who battled depression all their lives. But there has never been a saint who was not surrendered in extraordinary · measure to what Jesus Christ wanted to do and to express in his or in her particular, individual, unique human personality.

The challenge: self-expression

In concrete terms, the challenge to be "full of grace" is a challenge to *give expression* to the grace that is within us. **To surrender fully to God means to let God express Himself as He desires in and through our human actions.** It means that in word and deed we become a constant revelation of the light, the love, the life of Jesus Christ that is ours by participation; the life that is within us through our union with Him in grace. The challenge to be "full of grace" is a challenge just to be ourselves, provided that we understand "ourselves" to mean ourselves as joined to Jesus Christ in grace, and understand "to be" as meaning to let all that we are by grace express itself in and through our human actions.

To be "full of grace" is to be a mediator of the light and love and life of Christ to others. It is to be totally surrendered and sacrificed to all that Jesus Christ wants to do in and through us at any given moment -- and what He wants to do is give life, and give it in abundance to anyone who will receive it (see John 10:10).

We mediate the life of Christ to others through one thing: self-expression. To let our graced self express itself without fears, reserves or restrictions is to surrender our humanity to Christ to be the medium of His self-expression on earth. And His self-expression is that which gives life to the world. From Bethlehem to Calvary, the history of our salvation is the history of the Word of God expressing Himself in human flesh.

In practice this means to express freely our faith, our hope, our love. It means to let Jesus express His truth, His goals and desires, His confidence, His trust, His love through us. It means to let Him express Himself in us in deeds as well as in words, with passion as well as with restraint. This is to make grace visible, which is to give flesh to God.

To offer our bodies to be the transparent medium of Christ's self-expression on earth is a priestly dedication. It is to be "priests in the Priest" and "victims in the Victim" as members of the body of Christ our Head, who as Priest offered His own self as Victim for the life of the world. It is a deep dying to self -- to all selfishness, all self-protectiveness, all self-conscious reserve. It is to offer our flesh, as Jesus offered His on the cross, to bring the life of God to all we live and deal with -- all day, every day, holding nothing in reserve.

On a day-to-day basis, the key word that will help us do this is *expression*. We die to ourselves by joining in the singing at Mass as an expression of faith and worship. We die to ourselves by expressing our thoughts about God, about Jesus, to our children and friends when something within us wants to keep them very private. Or by praying out loud with others in our own words when we are embarrassed to do so. We die to ourselves when we express love and devotion to Christ when we are afraid it may make us look foolish. In other words, we die to ourselves by letting our true selves -- our graced selves -- appear in order to give life to the world, just as God the Son let His true self appear in the flesh and was crucified for it.

I know there is danger here for the imprudent. Some people just cannot judge what should or should not be expressed to others --

or to whom, or when, or where, or how. They "lay their religious trip" on others and turn everybody off. As a result, those who do have good judgment become over-reticent. They hold back from saying anything about their religion to anybody, or from any expression of devotion to God except in the privacy of their own hearts. Both extremes are wrong.

A simple way to start

A simple way to start mediating the life of Christ to others -- yet one which is immeasurable in its results --is this: *just resolve to express to all the people you meet everyday anything good you see in them.* And (most important) begin with the people you live and work with: especially, if you are married, your spouse and your children! It costs very little to give a compliment (a sincere one), yet we seldom do it. We are so afraid of looking bad ourselves if the compliment is not accepted that we won't take a chance on making someone else feel better. But how risky is it to say to a child when you come home from work, "I'm really glad to be back. You know, I missed you!" If your son shows consideration for someone else in the family, what do you lose by telling him you noticed how kind he was? What damage does it do to tell your daughter how pretty she is, or how nice she looks in something she is wearing?

And why not do the same thing for everyone you meet all day? The more conscious you are of Christ within you, the more conscious you become of what He sees in others, and what He rejoices in. Then you begin to see more and more good in others yourself. But you will not see very much, or see it very often, unless you begin to express it when you do.

To express love is to become more conscious of love. To become more conscious of love is to reaffirm it. To reaffirm love in yourself is to grow in love. And to grow in love is to give Christ's life to the world.

REFLECTION AND RESPONSE
to
"FULL OF GRACE"

SCRIPTURE : *Read:* Ephesians 1:1-10

PRAYER: Mary, you are full of grace. You are blessed among women. And in you we see embodied the fullness of that blessing which the Father has bestowed on us through Jesus your Son.

Mary, pray for me, that my surrender to your Son might be complete. I would like everything that is in me -- all my thoughts, words, appetites, actions and desires -- to be brought together into unity under His headship. I would like Him to be free to live and act and express Himself in me without resistance or reserves. Mary, pray for me that I might be full of grace. *Amen.*

OUR OBJECTIVE in this chapter is to accept ourselves as consecrated by grace **to mediate the life of God to others and to commit ourselves to doing it.** We do this by letting the light and love that are within us by grace find *expression* in our human words and actions.

The goal or ideal of our lives is to be "full of grace," which means to be totally surrendered to God who is dwelling within us, so that He can act and speak and express Himself through us in every way He desires -- not only without resistance, but with full cooperation from us who are His body on earth.

INVENTORY:
- What, up to now, did you think it meant to "be perfect?" What do you think it means now?

- How have you experienced helping people that only you could have helped, or in ways that only you could have done?
- On an average day, do you give more compliments or corrections to the people you live with? At work?

INPUT: • What helped me most in this chapter?
            • How can I best give expression to the life of God that is in me?

INITIATIVE:
- How can I live out this chapter in my life?
- When, where, and how will I do this?

PRAYER FORM FOR THIS CHAPTER: Say the rosary, but this time keep your attention on the meaning of the words. As you say them, however, be conscious of what they mean in the context of the mystery of the rosary that goes with each decade. For example, as you say "Hail Mary, full of grace, the Lord is with you" in the context of the Annunciation, when Mary learns she is chosen to be the mother of the Savior, that means one thing. The same words take on a different tone when addressed to Mary under the cross during the crucifixion of her Son. So speak the words of the *Hail Mary*`s to Mary, conscious of their meaning, but see her each time within the scene of the mystery that is assigned to each decade.

MANTRA: *say frequently during the day*: "Hail Mary, full of grace..."

CHAPTER SIX

MARY'S ASSUMPTION INTO HEAVEN

In 1950 Pope Piux XII declared it to be a dogma of the Catholic Church that Mary was taken up, body as well as soul, into heaven.

The question this immediately raises is not so much a theological question about whether or not the Assumption of Mary is a fact, or how it can be true, but the practical, pastoral question, "Why bother to define it?" The doctrine was not the subject of any furious debate in the Church. There were no conflicting opinions about it which demanded to be cleared up. In fact, there didn't seem to be a great deal of interest in this doctrine one way or another. So why did Pope Pius XII bother to declare it a defined dogma of the Church?

One wonders whether the answer is not more than the Pope himself was aware of. This doctrine is God's affirmation of the value of the body. In preserving the body of Mary from the corruption of the grave, God showed that the human body is not for Him just the wrapper of the soul -- something necessary during the time of one's earthly service, but which is just stripped off and thrown away when the soul is taken to heaven. The body is not just something we "use." It is us. And when Mary's work on earth was done, God didn't take her beautiful soul to heaven and leave her body to disintegrate in the grave. As a sign of the body's value to Him He took her, body and soul, into heaven.

When the Church declared Mary "Mother of God" it was to show that Jesus could not be divided. The Church refused to split Jesus into separate parts by saying that Mary was just the mother of His body, or of His humanity, but not of Jesus the whole person. Now, in defining the doctrine of the Assumption, the Church affirms again the fact that we, the body of Christ, cannot be divided. Human beings cannot be divided. We cannot make facile distinctions between the value of our bodies and the value of our souls. Or between what we do with our bodies and what we intend in our hearts. We cannot wholly separate our external expression from our interior response. We stand before God as whole persons, body and soul.

It is true that when we die, God allows a separation. Our bodies will go into the grave and disintegrate while our souls are taken to heaven. Why is this?

Death: the revelation of sin

Death came into the world with sin. The visible disintegration of our bodies at death is a sign of the invisible disintegration of our souls -- of ourselves as free persons -- which takes place every time we sin. Death lets us see what sin is.

When we sin we close our eyes. We shut down our mind's awareness of what we are doing, of how bad it is. Or we rationalize and deny that it is bad at all. In order to sin we normally blind ourselves to reality. So God in His mercy gives us something we cannot blind ourselves to, something which tells us very vividly what life is and what sin is. When we see the human body disintegrating before our eyes at death, we are forced to think both about life and about what sin does to the integrity of our persons. To expose the deceitfulness of sin God gives us death. And to make sure we understand He explains to us in revelation that it was through sin that death came into the world (see Romans 5:12).

As long as there is sin in the world we need death. Otherwise we might forget what life is all about.

It is true that Jesus came to destroy death. Our Lord overcame both sin and death through His own death on the cross, He did not remove death from the world, however, anymore than He removed sin. He took the sting out of death; He changed human death from defeat into triumph by making it the entrance into everlasting life and total joy (see 1 Corinthians 15:55). But until the time of His own final triumph at His second coming, the work of redemption is not complete. It is still the time of response. People are being called to believe and accept the Gospel. It is a time of invitation, of response and of freedom. Grace is at work in the world, and sin continues to work. And while they are both at work, the visible reality of death continues to reveal what sin is and what it does to human integrity.

Two timeframes

Here we encounter again the Christian understanding of time. (We considered this above, in the chapter on the Immaculate Conception). We speak in two timeframes at once: that of eternity, in which all is present now; and that of this earth, in which there is a before and an after, and in which what for God already is, for us has not yet come to be.

Seen from the vantage point of eternity, Jesus finished His work on earth. When He died on the cross He cried out to the Father, "It is consummated. I have finished the work you gave me to do" (see John 17:4 and 19:30). And in fact, even within the timeframe of this world Jesus did finish the work He was sent to do in His own humanity, acting in the body He received from Mary. But within the timeframe of this world the *total* work of Jesus is not complete. The work of salvation is still going on. The Kingdom has not yet been finally established. Before Jesus ascended into heaven He sent His apostles out to carry on His mission: to make disciples of all nations and to labor in His vineyard until His return. The time between Christ's ascension into heaven and His second coming is for the Church a time of labor, a time for bringing about the Kingdom. It is a time of stewardship, and fidelity is shown through persevering effort to establish the lifegiving reign of Christ over every area and activity of human life on earth. To be faithful stewards of the kingship of Christ means to struggle perseveringly against the power of sin and death until He comes again. For as long as Christ is at work in the world, sin and death are also at work. To labor as Christ's body on earth means to confront sin and death, both in the world and in our own selves, and let the power of Jesus triumph over them.

This is where the doctrine of the Assumption comes in to give clarity to our faith and strength to our hope. By preserving Mary's body from the corruption of the grave, God showed both His power and His will to deliver, not just His Son but the whole human race from the domination of death. Mary's Assumption is a persuasive sign that the Resurrection of Jesus applies to us.

But the disintegrating, destructive effect of sin on us which is revealed in death is also revealed in the disintegration of the social order, in sin's destructive influence on society and all human institutions. Christ's power over death, therefore, is also a power over all that corrupts society, disintegrates the human race, fragments us into a divided world of nation against nation, race against race, class against class. Jesus came, not only to free individuals from the domination of sin and death, but also to redeem human life on earth: to "bring everything in heaven and on earth together in unity under His headship." Mary's Assumption, then, is also a sign that Christ will triumph over all the disintegrating effects of sin in the "body politic;" that is, in human society.

A counterpart to the Immaculate Conception

The doctrine of the Assumption is a natural counterpart to the doctrine of the Immaculate Conception, and the parallelism between the two brings out the meaning of each. The Immaculate Conception shows us Christ's power over sin. He exempted His mother from Original Sin and from all the power that was in the environment to corrupt her attitudes and values. By baptism He emancipates us from that same power. But where Mary was *preserved* from all sin, we must be gradually *purified*. Although we are emancipated and freed, we still have to struggle courageously in the timeframe of this world against the power of sin until we come into the total freedom of the children of God. The Immaculate Conception is a sign of Christ's absolute power over sin that helps us believe and hope in the eventual total victory of His power over all the effects of sin in us.

In the same way, the doctrine of the Assumption shows us Christ's power over death -- and by extension over all that disintegrates human life on earth; that is, over all the corrupt and corrupting institutions, movements, philosphies or policies of human society. Jesus exempted His mother from the corruption of death as a sign that He has emancipated the world and everything in it -- every area and activity of human society -- from the power of death and disintegration. But just as we have to be gradually purified of sin while Mary was preserved from all sin, so the world has to be gradually purified from all disintegration and all that diminishes human life on earth -- and the preservation of Mary's body from disintegration and corruption is a sign of Christ's will and power to do this. It helps us to believe that we are *empowered to transform the world* and gives us the *hope* we need to persevere in our efforts to bring every area of human life and activity under the lifegiving reign of Jesus Christ.

A sign of power

In all this the focus is not really on Mary. It is on the power of Christ and the mystery of His power in us, His power at work in the world. Mary is a sign of the power of grace. The Immaculate Conception shows that Jesus has power, not only to preclude all domination of sin over the body He received from Mary, the body that was divine through its very being as the body of the Word made flesh, but also to purify from sin the body He took to Himself when He made us His members in baptism, the body that is made divine by grace. This is the body in which His words are only made flesh in the words of our own free choices. The Immaculate Conception promises and shows the power of Christ's grace to purify us because the body of Mary that was preserved from all sin was no different from ours; it was a human body made divine only by the gift of grace.

In the same way, the Assumption shows that Jesus has the will and the power to deliver our bodies from death. By preserving from corruption the body of His mother, a body made divine by grace exactly as ours are, He revealed to us the destiny that is ours and the destiny we must believe in for the world. Death's power over us has been broken. The head of the serpent whose strangling coils are intertwined with every institution in our society has been crushed. The victory has been won; it is up to us to extend it to all creation.

The significance of the Assumption today

Why did Pope Piux XII bother to define the dogma of the Assumption? Whatever his personal intention was, I believe that the decision to define this dogma when he did was a prophetic act.

The Assumption was proclaimed as a dogma in 1950. There is no escaping the significance of the historical context in which this definition was made. World War II was just over, a war that began with Hitler and ended with Hiroshima and Nagasaki. In Hitler's Germany eleven million human bodies in the concentration camps were exploited, starved, tortured, gassed to death, mined for usable materials such as hair and dental fillings, then cremated. About half of them were Jews. In the bombing of Hiroshima by the United States, the first nuclear attack in the history of the world, close to 100,000 human bodies were destroyed, many of them instantly vaporized. In the subsequent raid over Nagasaki, the city with the largest Christian population in the orient, an American Catholic pilot seized the only landmark he could find in a cloud-covered sky and dropped a second atom bomb on the Urakami-Nagasaki Cathedral. Over ninety thousand people died, including three entire religious orders of native Japanese nuns. After World War II, human bodies would never exist on earth again under the same terms as before. [1]

An age of torture

Then came the massive disregard of human rights and of the dignity of the human body

---

[1] I know of no book in which the story of Nagasaki has been better presented to the Christian conscience than Fr. Charles McCarthy's *August 9*, available from Box 5221, Station A, Portland, Maine 04101. McCarthy includes the conversion experience of Fr.George Zabelka, who was Catholic chaplain on Tinian Island with the Air Force group who dropped the atom bomb.

by one political regime after another which made torture a mainstay of "national security." The French in Algeria used on the Algerians the same tortures the Gestapo had used on the French. The Americans in Viet Nam used on the Viet Cong the same tortures the Communists were using on their prisoners. And almost every rightwing dictatorship in Central and South America makes a mockery of human rights through the torture and political assasination of dissidents, not to mention the massacre of entire villages by anti-insurgency forces, some of whom are trained and equipped by the United States. Because those whom we consider a threat to our "national security" show no respect at all for human rights or for the sacredness of the human body, the United States supports and equips other governments who show no more respect than they do. Whoever is the winner in all this, the human body is the loser. On both sides of warring factions today, no matter where or over what issues the fighting is going on, there seems to be nothing but contempt shown for human flesh.

The cheapening of sex

And in the midst of all this came what the journalists tagged "the sexual revolution." Everywhere the young people in our society look they get the message that there is nothing sacred about the body or about its sexual expression. Business executives proclaim through their advertisments that the female body can be displayed and exploited for the sake of sales. The proprietors of respectable neighborhood stores make a place on their shelves -- or sometimes under the counter -- for porn magazines. The TV and movie industries have dropped all pretense of maintaining a serious code of decency.

In the media, even the productions that are considered moderate seem to be based on a common assumption that the human body has no real value and its sexual expression is meaningless. Physical death and physical sex as they appear on the adventure-time screen are equally unreal: neither has any consequences; neither means anything. Lovers copulate as casually as the cowboys shoot each other in the westerns. In the movies, what you do to the body or with the body just doesn't count. This is Hollywood, but it isn't the real world. In the real world people who are shot to death don't get up and appear again in the next movie. And in the real world people who go to bed together cannot just walk away from it and be their previous selves again two hours later when the fun is over.

The message is reaching the youth. Teens are reciting the slogan, "It's okay if you love each other" as gullibly as if it were their folk heritage. Premarital sex among teenagers is taken for granted. And the price? The devaluation of the body. Sex doesn't mean what it did. The physical gift of one's body in intercourse doesn't have the same value it once did. Intercourse is no longer understood to be the expression of the total gift of one's self forever. It is just an expression of affection -- of the kind of "love" that accepts intimacy with this or that person for awhile, or for as long as the relationship endures.

The result of this has been an epidemic of pregnancies, of course. And unwanted pregnancies lead to unwanted babies -- who become a social problem. As a result, we as a nation have declared that the living human body has no value for us and no rights until it comes out of the mother's womb. And so we perform over a million abortions a year and dispose of the remains as coldly and inhumanly as the Nazis disposed of the bodies they "terminated" in their death camps. The ovens of Dachau and Auschwitz were the Nazis' "Final Solution" to what they referred to as the "Jewish problem." The garbage cans of the abortion clinics are the "final solution" our society offers to the problem of unwanted pregnancy.

Between 1973 and 1987 fifteen million babies were disposed of by abortion in the United States. Every year we violate and throw into the abortion clinic garbage ten times as many human bodies as were destroyed in the nuclear holocausts of Hiroshima or Nagasaki. And this is a characteristic of our times: massive disrespect for the body, massive contempt for human flesh, a massive attempt to make a separation between the human body and the human person. We pretend that we can destroy a human body in its mother's womb without assault on a person. We pretend that we can loan our bodies in uncommitted sexual intercourse without losing the integrity of our persons. We pretend that we can violate the human rights of others without becoming inhuman ourselves -- and that for the sake of "personal" and "spiritual" values like "freedom" we can torture and massacre human flesh in defense of our national security without losing the very soul of our nation in the process. All this is based on the myth that the human body can be dealt with in separation from the human person who is its soul.

The doctrine of the Assumption affirms the value of human flesh. God took the mother of His Son into heaven body as well as soul. But by extension, the doctrine of the Assumption also affirms the value and importance of everything physical, everything that belongs to or contributes to physical, bodily human existence on this earth. The Assumption proclaims that God is not just interested in getting us out of the world and into heaven, but that He wants our human existence on this earth to be respected, enhanced and fulfilled.

God's love for this world

The great German Jesuit Karl Rahner distinguished between God's *transcendent* love for us and His *cosmic* love. By His transcendent love, God calls us beyond this world to the life and joys of heaven. In His transcendent love God gives us grace, which is a sharing in

His own divine life over and above the level of human life which is ours by nature. [1]

But God also loves us with a cosmic love. This is God's love for us in this world, by which He desires for us the fullest, happiest life on this earth that is possible. In His cosmic love God wants every human institution and activity to be everything it can be and to contribute all it can contribute to the fullness of human life on earth. In His cosmic love God cares about business and politics, about health care, poverty, housing and education. In His cosmic love, God wants to bring under His lifegiving reign, not only those areas of human life which we recognize as being more directly concerned with "spiritual" or eternal values, but also what we sometimes call the "temporal order": all of those values and benefits of human living which will not last beyond the end of the world. God doesn't want us just to have and enjoy those things which will help us get to heaven. He wants us to have and enjoy ev-

---

[1] Rahner explains the distinction between God's transcendent love and His cosmic love in "Reflections on the Theology of Renunciation," and in "The Ignatian Mysticism of Joy in the World," which are both chapters in his *Theological Investigations III*.

erything that will make us happy, both here and hereafter.

That is why we are called, as stewards of the kingship of Christ, to *take responsibility for reforming, renewing and transforming every area of human life and activity on earth*. Every Christian who has understood the reign of God says with the Roman poet, "Nothing human is irrelevant to me": *nihil humanum mihi alienum puto*. Our mission is to bring everything human to its fullness.

The Assumption: sign of hope

The Assumption of the Blessed Virgin Mary into heaven gives clarification to our faith and strength to our hope as we face the task of renewing and transforming the social structures of this world.

The Assumption clarifies our faith by standing before us as a visible sign of God's concern for the body, for human flesh -- and by extension for everything that is physical and earthly. The fact that God took Mary, body as well as soul, into heaven is a proclamation that God is not just concerned about "spiritual" values or the spiritual wellbeing of His children. God is concerned about everything human, and about every human need, physical as well as spiritual. And so the doctrine of the Assumption, by focusing our attention on God's love for the body, draws our attention out by extension to everything cosmic, everything that touches, enhances, or diminishes human life on this planet. The Assumption makes it clear that Christians must be concerned about this world and accept as their responsibility and their mission the task of renewing it.

The Assumption strengthens and encourages us in this task by giving support to our hope. The dissolution and disintegration of the social order at times seem as inevitable as death. All around us we see corruption -- in family life, social life, business and politics. There are also encouraging elements, but too much of the time what we are most aware of is the hopelessness of it all. The power of sin seems to put the curse of death on every effort to renew the institutions of this world. Every surge of idealism seems short-lived, while self interest goes on forever. The disintegration of the social order seems to be as much a part of human life on earth as the disintegration of the body at death. There is just too much selfishness at work.

When we look at the wreckage of our social institutions we are tempted at times to succumb to the same disillusionment that Philip Caputo experienced during the Viet Nam war. Caputo was an idealistic volunteer enlistment, a Catholic college student, who left Loyola University in Chicago to go to Viet Nam with the Marine Corps and save the world from Communism. In his book *A Rumor of War*, he describes how the sight of blown-up and corrupting human bodies pulled the plug on his faith. When he saw them he knew: "These bodies will never rise again." It was not a logical conclusion -- all death, any death disintegrates the body more completely than what Caputo saw -- but the emotional impact of the vivid reality of death was just too much for him. He could no longer believe in the power of Christ.

I believe that what Philip Caputo saw was for him, consciously or not, more than the wreckage of bodies. I think his whole experience of the war, as he describes it with penetrating insight in his book, caused him to see there the wreckage of his own idealism. He saw the corruption of society, of institutions, of human life, of all he thought he was fighting for. It was not just the resurrection of the body he could no longer believe in; it was the resurrection of society. It was the resurrection of his own hope. He lost faith, not only in Christ's power to overcome death, but in His power to overcome sin -- the sin that corrupts or threatens to corrupt every institution and movement in human society. When it comes to human efforts and idealism, Christ's power over sin and His power over death (the effects of sin) go together. If we cannot believe in the one, we cannot believe in the other.

By preserving His mother's body from corruption, Christ has given us an enduring sign, not only of His power to raise our bodies from the dead, but to raise up society itself out of any corruption into which it may fall. It is this power which gives us hope and animates our zeal. And that is why the Assumption of Mary's body into heaven is the banner that rallies us to go out and renew the earth.

REFLECTION AND RESPONSE
to
THE ASSUMPTION OF MARY INTO HEAVEN

SCRIPTURE : *Read:* Matthew 12:46-50

PRAYER: Mary, you were the one most united to the heart of your Son, most supportive of Him in the work He longed to accomplish. And He has made us, like you, the intimates of His heart.

Mary, pray for me that I will not fail your Son. I know that the will of the Father is that the lifegiving reign of Christ's love should be established over every area and activity of human life on earth. Mary, work with me as you worked with His first apostles. Be the guide and support of my apostolate. Pray for me and help me transform the world for your Son. *Amen.*

OUR OBJECTIVE in this chapter is to understand and accept our mission **to transform the world as stewards of the kingship of Christ.** The taking of Mary's body into heaven shows us the respect, the concern God has for our bodies, for everything that belongs to human life and dignity here on earth. It calls us to reverence for the human body and to concern for the physical welfare of our brothers and sisters throughout the world.

The doctrine of the Assumption tells us that Jesus exempted His mother's body from corruption as a sign of His power over death -- and over all that disintegrates human life on earth -- and that we are sent with Christ's power to reform everything that disintegrates or diminishes human life on earth.

INVENTORY:
- What signs do you see in our society of disrespect for the human body?

- What efforts do you see being made in our country or by our country to bring about more respect for the body?
- What have you yourself done to improve the physical welfare of people close to you or far away?

INPUT: • What helped me most in this chapter?
        • What most needs changing in our own immediate environment? How can we help each other do something about it?

INITIATIVE:
- How can I live out this chapter in my life?
- When, where, and how will I do this?

PRAYER FORM FOR THIS CHAPTER: At some time when you can be alone -- for example, when you take your shower -- look back over the day, asking what changes of mood you experienced. Did you pass from happy to sad? From sad to happy? From peaceful to disturbed? From disturbed to peaceful, etc.?

• Then, ask what caused the change of mood. Was it a decision you made right before that? An event you responded to, either with a choice or just emotionally? Was it a thought that came into your head?

• Finally, ask what God might be saying to you in all of this? What, down deep, do you think your decision should have been? How, down deep, do you think you should have responded to this event, that thought? What does sadness or disturbance tell you? What does joy or peace tell you?

• In all of this, pay particular attention to thoughts or opportunities you may have had to do something that would change your environment and make it more according to the ideals and values of Christ. (If you like,

133

you can make this prayer a part of your daily life from now on.)

MANTRA: *say frequently during the day*: "Thy kingdom come!"

CONCLUSION: *This is our last chapter. If you want to continue with another book by the same author, several are available. In particular, there are a series of books based on the Gospel of Matthew which develop in greater depth and from Scripture each of the practical commitments which in this book we have seen following from the doctrines on Mary. For information write or call His Way Communications, c/o the Monastery of St. Clare, 1310 Dellwood Ave., Memphis TN 38127 (901-357-6662).*